Security Litigation

Best Practices for Managing and
Preventing Security-Related Lawsuits

Security Litigation
Best Practices for Managing and Preventing Security-Related Lawsuits

Eddie Sorrells

AMSTERDAM • BOSTON • HEIDELBERG • LONDON • NEW YORK • OXFORD
PARIS • SAN DIEGO • SAN FRANCISCO • SINGAPORE • SYDNEY • TOKYO

Butterworth-Heinemann is an Imprint of Elsevier

Acquiring Editor: Tom Stover
Editorial Project Manager: Hilary Carr
Project Manager: Punithavathy Govindaradjane
Designer: Greg Harris

Butterworth-Heinemann is an imprint of Elsevier
The Boulevard, Langford Lane, Kidlington, Oxford OX5 1GB, UK
225 Wyman Street, Waltham, MA 02451, USA

Notices
Knowledge and best practice in this field are constantly changing. As new research and experience
broaden our understanding, changes in research methods, professional practices, or medical treatment may become necessary.

Practitioners and researchers must always rely on their own experience and knowledge in evaluating
and using any information, methods, compounds, or experiments described herein. In using such
information or methods they should be mindful of their own safety and the safety of others, including
parties for whom they have a professional responsibility.

To the fullest extent of the law, neither the Publisher nor the authors, contributors, or editors, assume
any liability for any injury and/or damage to persons or property as a matter of products liability,
negligence or otherwise, or from any use or operation of any methods, products, instructions, or ideas
contained in the material herein.

ISBN: 978-0-12-801924-5

British Library Cataloguing-in-Publication Data
A catalogue record for this book is available from the British Library

Library of Congress Cataloging-in-Publication Data
A catalog record for this book is available from the Library of Congress

For information on all Butterworth-Heinemann
visit our website at http://store.elsevier.com/

Working together
to grow libraries in
developing countries

www.elsevier.com • www.bookaid.org

Almost 25 years ago, DSI Security Services took a huge risk and decided to hire a 21-year-old with no real future prospects. I am eternally grateful to Alan Clark and the entire Clark family for allowing me to be a part of this incredible adventure, and their family.

Anything I have ever accomplished, or will ever achieve in the future, is a direct result of the love and support of my wife. Thank you Stacie for your unyielding belief in me.

To my children Alex, Regan, and Peyton: You will always be my greatest work.

To my Father and Mother: Thank you for teaching me life and legal lessons far greater than those found in any book or classroom.

Contents

Introduction

As I set upon the adventure of writing this book, a glance around my office, and a quick Google search, told me that there were already a number of well-written and informative works on the topic of private security and the law. While it's debatable whether or not our industry needs more in the way of academic legal writing to inform and educate the practitioner, my goal was to write a different type of book. I have come to realize that the kind of book I could offer to our industry was one that is hopefully unique in its purpose and its scope. As I approach the milestone of celebrating 25 years in contract security, I have a wealth of experiences and stories that constantly bring to mind how critical the intersection of the law and the services we provide really is. I envision myself as a middleman – a security practitioner, a businessman, a licensed attorney, and an in-house counsel for a large contract security firm. While I have never wavered on what my professional and ethical duty is, or to whom my true loyalty is owed, I must admit that from time to time I have struggled with making sure that I am acting in the best interests of all involved. Add to this the fact that at the end of the day we are all in the customer service business and must act with this goal in mind, the multitude of hats I wear can cause my head to grow very weary and I often feel the overwhelming burden of having to always make the right calls at the right time. This has forced me to be not only a competent attorney, but also a trusted business adviser, security professional, and when humanly possible, a loyal vendor. If I've learned anything over the years it is that these roles can sometimes bring about a very delicate balance.

Quite often when I speak to various groups on legal topics I am asked very routine and straightforward legal questions. As I am providing the answer in a legally relevant manner, the security practitioner inside of me is always fighting to supplement most answers with "but that depends on …," followed by a personal story from a real-world customer experience. There are countless times where I've seen the services that we provide, the interest of our customers, and the law collide. It is that unique perspective I wanted to bring to this work. I have a view from all three sidelines: attorney, security practitioner, and company representative. On most days I wear all hats very comfortably, but on others I am not sure which has the best fit. It is an ongoing dilemma, but one that can be properly managed.

I did not intend to write an academic work on the latest case law dealing with private security, nor will you find on the following pages an exhaustive list of legal terms and theory accompanied by a detailed explanation of each. Again, these books and resources already exist and will hopefully continue to exist since they serve a great purpose and have assisted me many times over the years. Who knows, that may be my next literary challenge, but for now I truly felt that I needed to capture the spirit of countless conversations I have had with colleagues over the last several years concerning how the law impacts the services we provide. Not just what the law teaches, but what we learn in real life. I once had a law school professor tell me just prior to graduation that the law can teach you a lot about life, but life can teach you much more about the law. That has proven itself to be true time and time again. I love the law and I have great respect for its impartiality and the stability it brings to our society. But I also know that to understand it completely, it must be viewed through many different subjective elements just like any other area of life. It is also not my goal to offer instructions on how you should run your business or secure your clients; there are other books for that as well. But rather I hope to point out how these tasks can impact your ability to defend yourself, or your customer, when the lawsuit comes.

I have attempted to use real-life examples that I have encountered throughout my career to illustrate what can happen and how unpredictable the process can often be. Each scenario is factual and comes from cases or incidents that actually occurred. Through each I learned some things I should have been doing differently, and some things I should have never done. I hope that my experiences can assist you in approaching how to manage liability risks and deal with litigation when you encounter it. I would also point out that any advice that is offered in the pages of this book is done so in a general sense without regard to individual state laws on torts, discovery rules, or other controlling authorities that will govern many actions in lawsuits. As always, make sure you are consulting an attorney before making any drastic decisions. It should also be noted that often the decisions that have to be made are not easy ones and turn on issues such as risk management and company philosophy. I am rarely quick to criticize competitors, colleagues, or customers for making decisions that may differ from my own. They may be dealing with a totally different set of internal and external dynamics than what I have in front of me. No two events are ever identical and can only be successfully approached after conducting a "big picture" evaluation of all the facts.

Before we start the adventure of talking about the all too real world of security litigation, let's take a closer look at our industry. The contract security business has never been stronger. The global demand for private contract security services is expected to increase each year eventually reaching $244 billion in 2016.[1] As our customer base expands, so do the challenges. Currently, there is not a uniformed set of standards in our industry and each company must chart its own course to set internal rules and ensure compliance with differing regulations that vary from state to state. In the last 15 years ASIS International has published guidelines in a variety of areas including risk assessments and security officer training and selection criteria, but there remains a void when attempting to establish what is the recognized "standard" or benchmark to measure how we conduct our business.[2] And while there are a multitude of great companies in our industry, large and small, that conduct their operations with great care and set for themselves high ideals that must be met in critical areas, the absence of any recognized and validated best practices often puts or professional reputations in a negative light. This is one reason I believe that we are often targets for litigation. And don't be fooled into thinking that just because there are no real "national standards" that there will not be any benchmarks that will be used in attempt to show that you deviated from what a "professional" security company would have

---

[1]World Security Services Study, The Freedonia Group http://www.freedoniagroup.com/industry-study/2978/world-security-services.htm

[2]In June 2015 the ASIS International Standards and Guidelines Commission voted to pursue a standard in the Area of Security Officer Selection and Training. The process is expected to take up to 2 years.

done. Often this is accomplished through utilizing expert testimony from industry veterans who will craft what standards should be followed when securing the customer's environment. These problems will likely only become tougher as our industry expands and society's appetite for violence increases.

There are a few areas that may warrant a passing mention but will not be a major focus in the pages that follow. While proprietary security forces are decreasing as more industries see the value in contracting this vital function to professional companies whose sole focus is the security program, they remain a large part of the security world. Because of my experiences, and I think the need for more education in this area, the vast majority of the material will focus exclusively on contract security services. However, with the exception of the obvious mentions concerning how to deal with a customer entity, much of the information you will find is just as applicable to the process of managing proprietary forces. They are held to the same standards in regards to negligence and providing reasonable measures as the contract industry is.

There are also certain types of actions that will not be prominently featured. There are a multitude of legal actions that companies in the security industry should expect to deal with on a routine basis. One such area is Workmen's Compensation. In terms of real numbers, Workmen's Compensation cases will likely take up the largest percentage of the legal actions you face year-to-year. These matters can be complex and troubling, but for the most part they are not extremely unique and don't often result in large financial awards and long protracted trials. And while certain chapters do address the customer dynamics that arise when contract security officers are injured, there will not be an exhaustive focus on this area of law.

I can also guarantee that if you have been engaged in this industry for virtually any length of time, you have likely been hit with either a state or federal action alleging some type of workplace discrimination or wage and hour issue. This can be an extremely serious issue and employment law matters should never be taken lightly, especially in the era of increasing class actions and intense focus on security providers in states such as California. But ultimately I felt that the greatest contribution of this book should be in areas that routinely pose the biggest threat to all companies involved in security services.

Negligent security, also called inadequate security or premises liability cases, is a cause of action that strikes at the very heart of what we do. It is a direct attack on what we seek to supply and the promises we make to our customers. It is a sobering experience to read count after count that utilize words such as "failed to" or "negligently" to describe the actions of our companies and customers. And no other type of case forces us to more fully evaluate our policies and procedures than when we are forced to use the plaintiff's microscope to examine every minute detail of the business operations. I would estimate that on a least 100 different occasions during my career I have enacted what I call new "lawsuit" rules. These are new procedures, or modifications made to existing policies, that came about after learning a lesson during a lawsuit. It is truly an evolutionary process. Just when you think you have every conceivable rule and process in place to protect your business, along comes a plaintiff who shows you all the areas that are truly exposed. This will never end, and if there can be a silver lining to getting sued, it may be that it allows us another shot at fixing something that may have been lurking for years prior to being exposed.

These types of lawsuit are also where the biggest challenges arise in the customer relationship. In preparing to write this book, I spoke to a few attorneys to get advice and guidance on how to approach the subject. I explained that I wanted to depart from a straightforward academic endeavor, and venture into areas that may ultimately even be at odds with the law. I could almost hear some of them question my sanity and the value of a book that did not reinforce the need to protect your own legal interests at all costs. Lawyers are trained to be zealous advocates for their clients and it is antithetical to everything they professionally value to entertain doing anything that may assist another party at the expense of their client. But this question may have to be explored by a businessman, or even an in-house counsel, when it comes down to current or future customer prospects. I have been told many times by small security company owners that they have often been advised by their attorneys reviewing a proposed contractual agreement that they would be crazy to sign it. As one told me, "I had to decide if I would rather be crazy or broke." That's the real world, and unfortunately, it does not always match up to the one found in case law or scholarly articles. I hope that the pages that follow will help to bridge that gap.

I have been most fortunate to work with some of the finest security professionals in our industry, and I've also been blessed to work with some of the most experienced and qualified attorneys in the civil defense bar. I have learned that a reputable and trustworthy insurance broker and carrier is a security company's best friend. Thankfully I do not have a long list of horror stories about how I was victimized by someone who was less than competent in his or her ability to provide these services, and it is my sincere hope that nothing in this book is construed to cast a negative light on any of the aforementioned professionals. But based on my experiences, quite often there is a disconnect between these parties that requires knowing how to navigate potentially troubling waters. When I decided to take up the challenge of creating this work, I decided that the only true value to anyone that takes the time to read it would be through what I have learned in these situations – ups and downs, good and bad, and mistakes and triumphs. After reading this book, it is my hope that you will walk away with a different perspective, not just on how the law works and what your potential risks are, but on how to deal with the unique challenges faced by our industry. I hope in some small way you can gain some insight, guidance, and a little bit of advice on how to confront these issues when they land on your desk.

The contract security triangle (the company, the customers, and the plaintiffs)

"You're the expert-you tell me!" When I first heard those words as a young branch manager of a contract security company, I at once felt a rush of fear, mixed with accomplishment, spring forth in my mind. I had not been in the security industry for a long period of time, and as a young 24-year-old manager I was not sure I deserved the label of an "expert" in any area of my chosen vocation. But this abrupt response to a question I had posed to a potential customer about where he wanted his security officer stationed, made me feel an immediate sense of pride about my role in this process of providing him with what I thought would be a simple quote-after he told me exactly what he wanted. That feeling quickly vanished when I came to the realization that he was looking to me to not only provide the personnel to stand guard over his business, but I was also being called upon to give some level of expertise on how his security program should work. As I stumbled over words such as "Well, it depends how tight you want your access control to be," and "I will need to see your emergency evacuation plan first," I began to realize that the contract security industry is much more than simply supplying people to customers who use them as they wish. It is about providing a level of expertise to our customers that allow them to have a sense of confidence that they are receiving one of the most important services they will ever purchase. In hindsight, I would have been shocked if my future customer would have turned to me and said, "How do you think I should go about running my factory?" I would have quickly told him that I had no knowledge of operating a facility that produced paper goods, and I would have thought that he was a little misguided for asking. But for far too many security professionals, it is hard to comprehend that we are the experts who should be advising our customers on what they should be doing, and how it can be done.

Over the past 25 years, that conversation has often come to mind as I have sat in depositions while an overly aggressive plaintiff's attorney continually refers to me as an "expert" on topics such as security staffing, training, wage rates, and any other issue that can be used to inject doubt about the effectiveness of a particular security program. While it would be easy, and in some cases a better answer than some of the ones I have given, to simply say "I'm no expert, we're just the company they hired," I have come to learn it is not quite that simple. Every decision made, contract signed, post order produced, and training program developed, can and will play a part when litigation enters the picture. And as our industry grows, we have to be ready to confront these issues on a more frequent basis.

Every day in the United States, over one million security officers protect people, property, and countless other assets in a variety of environments.[1] Security officers outnumber sworn law enforcement personnel by a margin of two to one worldwide.[2] These dedicated men and women perform a vital role in protecting commercial properties, healthcare facilities, industrial sites, and serve as our nation's first line of defense at many critical infrastructure locations. Security officers are routinely responsible for securing access, patrolling property, and serve as the eyes and ears to intercept potential criminal activity and the ever-present threat of terrorism throughout our nation. It is anticipated that the private security industry will continue to grow as corporate America continues to seek competent and comprehensive solutions to protecting their assets. This growth will also bring with it an increase in security litigation and an analysis of every step of the contracting process.

I have been fortunate to work with some of the best defense counsel available in cases where we have found ourselves in the defendant's chair, but over the years I have found that one simple concept can sometimes elude them: You may be put in the position of fighting for yourself and your customer. This is never truer than when you find your customer is also in the defendant's chair because of an alleged lapse of security. I always begin by having a standard conversation with our outside counsel about the responsibility that I have, to effectively and vigorously defend my company from lawsuits; but at the same time, I make sure that we are upholding the

---

[1] US Bureau of Labor Statistics, Division of Occupational Employment Statistics, May 2011. National Estimate of 1,032,940 Security Officers. See http://www.bls.gov/oes/current/oes339032.htm

[2] "Private Security Fatalities Comparable to Police Fatalities," by Carlton Purvis. Security Management. January 17, 2013. See http://www.securitymanagement.com/print/11530

promise we have made to our customers. This can sometimes result in very tough decisions, and it is not a goal I can always achieve. Regardless of the philosophy of the security company, it is at minimum a complication that is always there in many situations.

THE CONTRACTING PROCESS

Before we can talk meaningfully about addressing the pitfalls of security-related litigation, we must first fully understand the relationship of our companies, our customers, and the potential plaintiffs. There are many reasons that companies, large and small, outsource their security functions to a third party. Whether it is supplying officers or some type of electronic security solution, most organizations have come to realize that a reputable security company can offer cost-effective solutions that offer a variety of benefits. For example, if the company is selective in who it hires to manage its security program, it can take full advantage of the security company's expertise, consulting services, and personnel management skills. This leaves the customer to do what it does best (manufacturing, healthcare, retail, etc.) without spending valuable time and other resources on an area where there may not be much "in-house" knowledge. Another benefit is to transfer some of the risks associated with security liability. While this is not always, and never should be, the sole reason to hire a third-party security firm, it is nonetheless an ever-present issue throughout the contacting process.

Most companies will follow a similar type of format when seeking proposals from security companies that often include a list of duties, officer qualifications, insurance requirements, and in some cases, contractual terms. This is where the groundwork for any potential litigation is laid. When incidents turn into lawsuits, questions such as: Who decided on how many officers to hire? Who decided if they would be armed or not? Did you offer to do a security assessment for your customer, and if so, did they refuse? are sure to be asked. So it is imperative to address them early in the relationship when dealing with a proposed contract. These questions may be factually simple, but can be difficult to address during litigation if you wish to maintain the relationship. How this situation can play out will be discussed in much more detail later, but for now, it is important to understand that going to battle in a security-related case is not always as simple as choosing sides. What if the plaintiff is your customer's employee? What if it is a third party, you were instructed to keep out? What if it's your own employee? I have been involved in many lawsuits over the years, and I don't remember ever having a situation where there was not at least one minor, or major, complication that could potentially have an impact on future customer relationships.

Before we go any further, let me address the obvious: contracts are rarely perfect for either side, and it is inevitable that one, or hopefully both, will have to assume more risk than they would like. I have come to realize that managing risks is an everyday task that never goes away. I am often asked to evaluate potential business to determine if the financial benefit to our company is worth the apparent risks that will likely be present throughout the life of a contract. I learned long ago that if I am waiting on an account that poses zero liability risks before we jump into a contractual relationship, I will spend an eternity waiting and our company will not last very long. They simply don't exist. The attorney in me is sometimes at war with the businessman, but at the end of the day our management team has to decide the level of risks that they are comfortable with. That is the real world that is not always taught in law schools or insurance seminars. No one ever trained me how to handle a situation where the other party responded to a well-drafted agreement by saying, "nice try, but we're not signing this." I have had dozens of well-meaning insurance professionals come to me over the years and suggest "standard" contractual clauses to be used to shield our company from any and all liability in a variety of situations. While the language may be legally sound, extremely well drafted, and will likely accomplish the stated purpose, it still has to be signed off on and agreed to by your customer – who most often also has a well-informed attorney looking to push as much risk as they can back to your side of the table. That is where the education truly begins.

Knowing which contractual provisions pose the most risk, and what type of risks, is of utmost importance from the outset of the relationship. This goes far beyond just running down a list of "what-ifs" when attempting to dream up worse case scenarios if something should go wrong during the course of service. It is having a fundamental understanding of some of the key concepts that can have a drastic impact on a lawsuit years in the future. Several years ago, I gave a presentation at the annual ASIS International Seminar and Exhibits about how security contracts play a major role in future litigation. During the Q&A, one of the attendees asked me a question and followed up by requesting that I answer as a "security professional and not a lawyer." Talking with him later, I realized that even though he had been in the industry for over 20 years, he still struggled with certain insurance and contractual issues because he had never gotten a "layman's" explanation. Some of the most common provisions are also the most misunderstood. We will dive into each of these in much more detail later, but for now, here is a basic understanding of what these concepts really mean.

INDEMNIFICATION

As a young security professional, many years before I made the decision to formalize my legal education, I had many experiences with the concept of indemnification. I can remember being asked to sign a hold harmless/indemnification agreement with a current customer and asking a more seasoned colleague what the word "indemnification" meant. He replied, "that just means they're legally responsible if they do something wrong, and we're legally responsible if we do something wrong." While that simple explanation satisfied me at the time, I have since learned that the concept of indemnification is far more complex and must be approached taking many different factors into consideration. Imagine my surprise after a particular incident occurred where all the facts pointed to the conclusion that our employees did nothing incorrect or legally negligent, only to find out later that this concept called "indemnification" may make us responsible for defending someone else who is in the crosshairs of a lawsuit, or paying an insurance loss. Situations can become further complicated when the duty to indemnify can literally turn on a few words or sentences in the lawsuit itself. Only by looking at these obligations at the contractual stage can you truly assess your potential risk and the future scenarios that may play out if or when you're involved in a lawsuit with your customer. Indemnification clauses in contracts are responsible for springing forth many lawsuits between security companies and their customers that no one sees coming.

In its simplest form, indemnification is the assumption of liability that otherwise would belong to someone else. That "someone else" could be your customer or a related entity. You, and in reality your insurance company, are essentially agreeing to cover the loss when a claim or lawsuit happens in the future. This could include payment of defense costs, investigative efforts, loss of product, and court judgments. Depending on how broad or narrow the indemnification obligations are, this could have dire consequences for the security contractor if they are agreeing to accept the majority, or in some cases all, of the responsibility for a loss.

ADDITIONAL INSURED

Another commonly misunderstood occurrence is the granting of additional insured status in a contract. This is also one way to provide the assurance of indemnification. The basic concept of granting someone additional insured status in itself is not extremely complicated and fairly easy to comprehend. Simply put, it means that the security company is allowing the customer to take advantage of the benefits of being an insured under their policy. This is primarily designed as a tool to allow the customer to be shielded from risk that may arise from or because of the security company's operations. This request is extremely common in security services contracts, and is not in itself a huge risk to either party. However, simple things such as other contractual terms and policy limitations can play a large role in future disputes. This is also one way that indemnification obligations are further secured. For example, if for some reason a security company does not honor the indemnification language in the contract, or the indemnification clauses is later proved to be unenforceable, the customer can attempt seek to the same protection under additional insured status.

SUBROGATION

It is a reoccurring nightmare for any businessman, much less anyone engaged in the security profession, to get the dreaded phone call that there's been some type of loss experienced by the customer. This can range from lost product, loss of equipment, or even injury to employees or visitors. Any such event requires an exhaustive investigation to find out the root causes and the responsible parties. It is always a somewhat satisfying moment to find out, at the conclusion of the investigation, that the customer does not hold the company or its employees responsible for such loss and even commends the security company on a job well done in how it handled or reacted to the incident. Case closed? Not so fast!

In the world of contract security the concept of subrogation is never far away. This is one of a few situations that is rarely contemplated when the relationships starts and the terms are being placed in the contractual agreement. It can be difficult to comprehend how a third party that has no contractual relationship with your company can now "stand in the place" of the damaged party and attempt to recover. Subrogation most often occurs in the private security world when there's a loss suffered by your customer, or third parties operating on your customer's premises, and an insurance claim is paid directly to one of those parties. The insurance company that paid the claim then begins to see if they can hold anyone else responsible to reimburse them for the claim. Depending on the state's statute of limitations, this can sometimes occur several years after the actual event. I can recall many occurrences where I have packed up my files on a particular case only to drag them out later when I get hit with a subrogation claim I did not see coming.

POTENTIAL PLAINTIFFS

"At least we can't get sued over this." I have heard this statement countless times over the years. This statement usually comes at the end of a long and dramatic explanation concerning some security event or a loss that occurred at a customer location, along with a list of facts that purport to show that "we" did nothing wrong. This is often followed up with a briefing on the various phone calls that have been made that resulted in firm assurances that we "don't have to worry about this one." While I have come to admire the naiveté that prompts such conclusions, and frankly I often wish I too had such an optimistic view of our legal system, but unfortunately these reports force me to begin the process of laying out scenarios of how a potential plaintiff could bring an action and how it could be defended.

In security litigation, potential plaintiffs can fit into four basic categories: (1) visitors to the customer's property, (2) customer employees (or residents in the case of residential litigation), (3) other vendors and contractors on the customer's property, and (4) the customer themselves. Each potential plaintiff group can bring a different set of legal issues. Depending on how contractual provisions are drafted, some very unique scenarios can present themselves in the course of service. The stereotypical plaintiff, who is seeking economic justice because they have been a victim of crime or some other perceived injury, is not always what you will find on the other side of the courtroom.

Recently, I received a call from one of our management employees who reported that he had just met with a customer who was very upset because we were "suing their company over an injury sustained by one of our officers." Knowing that any such litigation would be initiated by me, or at minimum I would've been aware of the action, I knew immediately there must be some misunderstanding. After several phone calls I determined that the customer had in fact received a letter putting them on notice that our employee intended to file a lawsuit for an alleged defect on the premises that caused his accident. As I attempted to reassure our client that it certainly is not good for business to go around suing our current customers, and that unfortunately I could not control what legal decisions our employee decided to make with respect to the threatened action, one thought popped into my head: What about the contract? As soon as that thought entered my mind, my customer verbalized the same concern – "Eddie, is there anything in our contract that prevents this from happening?" After some quick review of the contract and facts of the case, the simple answer was likely yes. While there was nothing in our agreement that could prohibit someone, in this case our employee, from filing a lawsuit, I did find a rather broad indemnification agreement that began to paint an interesting set of potential circumstances. Could we be put in the position of having to defend our customer even when the plaintiff is our own employee? Thankfully no such action ever commenced so the language was not tested, but you can be sure that there was a clear message sent that we would be looked at to "take the bullet" if one was ever filed.

These are just a few of the issues you must be aware of, in order to effectively navigate through the contracting process and ultimately security litigation. Throughout this book you will see that every situation is unique in its facts and circumstances, but certain truths hold firm in every situation. No matter the scenario, nothing is ever as simple as it may seem and you must be prepared for what may come. In order to proactively combat legal pitfalls down the road, you must begin now to widen your perspective and be willing to look at every conceivable angle of not only the contract laid before you, but also the future possibilities. No one can accurately predict the future, especially in the ever-changing environment of contact security, but it pays to be prepared. As we go on this journey, hopefully you will come to appreciate some of the steps that must be taken to protect you, and your customers, from serious trouble down the road.

I still remember getting a phone call several years ago from a very large customer after we had both been served with a lawsuit alleging various causes of action related to the level of security at one of their facilities. We both knew that we were about to experience a long journey of responding to requests for documents, endless motions, hearings being scheduled and rescheduled, and possibly a trial. While neither of us really blamed the other for what was taking place, we also knew that it was not going to be a positive turning point in our relationship. He ended the conversation with this: "Eddie, I'm glad we have an *expert* like you on our side to make sure we both come out of this case okay." Just as I had done 20 years earlier, when that word first entered my professional world, I hung up the phone feeling a little proud, but mostly humbled by the enormous expectation I knew it carried.

Who is the DECIDER? Risk assessments, industry standards, and operating procedures

Assumptions are the enemy of all things good. I am sure that this phrase did not originate with me, but I have used it countless times in my professional and personal life. I suffer from a condition, I refer to as "assumption syndrome." This is an affliction that causes me to assume that everyone knows what I know and has the benefit of my knowledge, experience, and expertise. They must know "this" and of course they know "that." These thoughts have littered my thinking on many occasions when I am debating how much information needs to flow from me to our employees and customers. Make no mistake; this attitude is not born out of arrogance or the feeling that someone who does not know what I do, is in some way inferior. It is actually quite the opposite. I just naturally assume that if I know something, surely everyone else is in on it. How could I possibly have any original pearls of wisdom to share with others that have not already been shared by another security expert at some point in the past? At one time, this would seriously impact my speaking engagements.

When I am asked to speak at an industry event, to a group of customer employees, or even our own team members, I always start by considering who the audience is. While this is probably a good trait for any effective speaker, who wishes to ensure that the topic is relevant and presented appropriately it also has caused me to occasionally second-guess my material. "I am sure they have heard that suggestion before" or "Everyone is aware of that new law" are statements that I use to convince myself that there is nothing new in this area. This occasionally resulted in a final presentation that was so elevated in its subject matter and approach that it would miss the audience all together. One such occasion changed my outlook and attitude for the better.

Several years ago, I was asked by a colleague to address a group of elite security professionals during a retreat. The topic I was assigned dealt with violence in the workplace and a disturbing new trend at that time known as Active Shooters. I thoughtfully prepared my presentation and a couple of weeks prior sent it to the committee that was overseeing the function. The feedback was extremely positive and I began to look forward to the session and the opportunity for a panel question and answer session immediately following. Then I got the email. A roster of attendees landed in my inbox just a few days before the event, and as I reviewed the list, I was struck with a sense of panic as it hit me for the first time that I would be presenting to a number of Chief Security Officers for literally the largest and most powerful companies in the world. The list was full of men and women who had impressive backgrounds in the FBI, Secret Service, along with distinguished careers in private security. It was only then that the internal dialogue started.

What could I possibly offer in the way of "new" information to a former secret service agent who has been a Chief Security Officer for a Fortune 500 company for over 10 years? Surely, he has had an occasion to examine the proper response to violence in the workplace. Are the things that I have to offer, that I consider somewhat routine and commonplace, of any value to a group such as this? It was too late to back out at the final hour so I decided to press on and try to be prepared for the inevitable underwhelming response my talk was sure to elicit. As I stepped on the stage a few days later and began to offer my knowledge and recommendations, I was immediately shocked at how well it seemed to be received. Instead of eye rolling and people remarking "who hired this lightweight," the presentation hit the target. As I stepped off the stage to begin the panel discussion, I was met by one of the industry giants I had assumed would think my words were a colossal waste of time. "Thanks so much for your presentation and if you have time I would love to talk with you more about how we can incorporate some of your suggestions at our locations." His remark, along with the explanation that people in his position did not always have the time and focus to devote to certain issues, finally made me realize that we all have a part to play, and regardless of what role we have, we should play it. While I still struggle occasionally with "assumption syndrome" flare ups, after that encounter it has mostly been in remission.

Words matter. Research tells us that the average person can often speak up to 20,000 words per day. Based on that volume, it is safe to assume that not everything we utter, whether it be in our personal or professional life, has some deep meaning or carries dire consequences if ignored, or accepted. But what about the written word? Does it somehow carry more meaning than something spoken? When it comes to litigation, the resounding answer is yes! And how the written word is created and conceived is sometimes just as important as the words themselves.

President George W. Bush stepped up to the White House podium on April 18, 2006 to take questions about continued speculation concerning the Secretary of Defense Donald Rumsfeld's future status in his administration. After being peppered with questions about how the critics of Secretary Rumsfeld had attempted to influence the president to make a change, President Bush responded, "I hear the voices, and I read the front page, and I know the speculation. But I'm the *decider*, and I decide what is best. And what's best is for Don Rumsfeld to remain as the secretary of defense."[1] I'm the decider. The buck stops with me. Despite the criticism of my detractors, or the adulation of my fans, I am the one who calls the shots. That was the message that President Bush was trying to convey in the midst of mounting calls for Rumsfeld's resignation, in reaction to what they viewed as the administration's failed policy in Iraq. And while this unique choice of words was instant fodder for late night comedians and political pundits, President Bush was making a point that is too often overlooked in business, and in life: somebody has got to take the responsibility for making a decision. All too often in security litigation no one wants to wear the label "the decider."

At the beginning of a security service relationship, some normal ground rules have to be established. These can include pay rates, bill rates, operating procedures, uniform styles, and equipment needs. But one of the most overlooked elements of beginning the security relationship is designing the security plan and procedures. This may seem to be a simple task, but there are many hidden areas that can cause significant issues for service providers, customers, and even insurance companies. One of the first questions that will be asked when litigation arises is: Who decided on what security measures were going to be implemented at this property? The answer can change the course of a security case and ultimately the legal survival of a party.

At a recent company function, I was speaking to a group of our managers about the liability risks associated with residential properties. These included an increased risk of crimes as compared to industrial settings, and other elements common to providing security services where people make their home. During this training, I reviewed several key areas of liability prevention and asked to be notified any time a residential account was being proposed or discussed, so that I could guide our risk management protocols accordingly. A week or so after my presentation, I was going through my mail and came across a new contract that had recently been acquired by a manager, who was present for my residential security briefing. As I reviewed the contract and accompanying documentation, it became apparent that this

---

[1]Bush: 'I'm the decider' on Rumsfeld. CNN April 18, 2006 http://www.cnn.com/2006/POLITICS/04/18/rumsfeld/

account fitted every definition of "residential services." Some quick research uncovered the fact that, despite outward appearances on the contrary, this location had experienced a fair amount of property damage, burglary, and other types of crimes. I also found that the property had been sold numerous times and had experienced financial difficulties. As the red flags continued to mount, I began to wonder why my directive concerning residential security services, that I had painstakingly outlined at our meeting just a couple of weeks before, had been ignored. When I contacted the manager who was responsible for the addition of this account, I got my answer: words.

"Don't worry about anything, this is a residential account, but we are not providing security services." This statement was intended to remove from mind any anxiety that normally is present when I hear the words "residential security," but what followed not only failed to set me at ease, but presented me with a whole new challenge. "Great," I replied, "what kind of services are we providing? "Concierge services," was the immediate response, and it was delivered with an assurance that the student had now somehow become the teacher. As I quickly began to ready my textbook definition of what I knew to be real "concierge services," I asked for a more detailed explanation of what these services would entail. "Making sure that the lobby is secure and everyone who visits a resident is stopped and asked to sign in," was his reply. After almost 25 years in this great profession, I was fairly certain that what he had just described would be deemed by anyone's estimation as what I had always known it to be; Security Services.[2] As I began to explain my feelings about the situation, I soon came to the realization that this otherwise well-qualified and intelligent business professional had fallen prey to accepting a carefully worded description of the proposed services offered by a prospect, even if it did not match reality. As he further explained that the customer had been very specific in wanting the services to be described as "concierge" rather than "security," I took him on a quick journey of how this word scramble would play out if litigation became a reality down the road.

When a potential customer reaches out to a security services provider, or if the provider is calling upon a prospect, at some point, the duties that the provider will accept responsibility for performing will, and should, come up. I have been somewhat surprised over the years at how often these discussions will lack any meaningful dialogue concerning what the property's security needs are, past experiences, and what assessments need to be performed in order to gauge the current risk level. Many times the *status quo* is readily

---

[2]Many security companies offer professional concierge services to residential properties and large office buildings. There is nothing inherently negative concerning the concept of providing or offering these services. But from a liability perspective, factors such as the duties of the security officers and post instructions will be the standard by which future responsibility will be measured-not necessarily how the service was described or labeled.

accepted and the real negotiation centers on financial concerns. The businesses that utilize our services, and our industry as a whole, deserve better. But when a legal situation develops, these early talks are not only important – they could potentially mean success or failure in a court of law. "How did you determine how many officers were going to be assigned to this property?" "How did you decide whether or not they would be armed or unarmed?" These questions have been asked of me countless times in depositions, and I truly wish I had a legally sufficient answer every time it had been. But too often I am left with pointing the proverbial finger at our customer, or one of our employees, who did not know any better.

So what is the best way to approach the question of who is the decider? The process must start early. It should be the centerpiece of the relationship from the very first meeting. Questions such as, "Have you done a recent risk assessment?" or "Tell me about the security issues you have faced at this property," should be common fixtures in any proposal process taken on by the security services provider. Even after spending more than half my life in the security services industry, I still learn lessons every day. Some can bring with them a sense of great joy over gaining a new nugget of wisdom, and some can be downright painful as the realization of missed opportunities sinks in. Such was the case that began with a heart-to-heart meeting with a local manager about a problem account.

In each business, the management team must constantly evaluate and re-evaluate the level of risk that they are comfortable with, and knowing the core philosophy of our company since its founding, the discussions concerning terminating a relationship with a customer happen very rarely and are only considered in cases of finances or an unforeseen extreme amount of risk. But on this particular afternoon, the team was discussing a residential complex that seemed to be becoming increasingly dangerous for our personnel, based on the recent events and staffing levels. You may be asking yourself: isn't that the type of environment that is in need of a security services company? With proper resources, staffing, and equipment, that would be true. But it was increasingly apparent to us that it would not be the case. So on this Friday afternoon, I told our local manager that first thing Monday, we would reach out to the customer and discuss our concerns and whether or not we wanted to continue the business relationship. As I woke that Sunday morning and began my ritual of flipping through the local news, my eyes were immediately drawn to a headline that included the name of the very customer we had spoken of less than 48 h earlier, and the words, *"College Student Shot and Killed."* I immediately contacted the manager, I had spoken to on Friday, to get all the details and he confirmed my worst fears. We had, in fact, been on the property when the alleged homicide occurred, and while it appeared that we had done all that we were supposed to do according to the post instructions, the tragedy happened nonetheless. Would additional security measures have made a difference? Could a frank discussion with our customer have prevented this outcome? As the facts began to unfold the answer to these hypotheticals was very likely no, but it reminded me once again of the importance of addressing vulnerabilities in our industry. And just as other conversations with managers have brought about teachable moments, this one did not disappoint in that regard either.

The week prior when we had discussed our concerns about this property, I had taken the time to research the history of this particular complex. After finding out that the name of the complex had changed at least once, I was somewhat surprised to find out, while not being overly shocked, that a double homicide had occurred there approximately 2 years earlier. After this recent tragedy, I brought this fact up to our manager during our Sunday morning conversation. His response reinforced an underlying misunderstanding of one of the most fundamental concepts of security litigation, especially in the residential realm: *Foreseeability*. "I had no idea about these issues when I sold the account, and man am I glad now that I never asked." As I began to reconstruct the scenario, it became very obvious that no discussion had ever taken place concerning the risks associated with the property, current challenges known by the property management, or at minimum the criminal history in or surrounding the premises. The tried-and-true concept of "out of sight, out of mind," does not always work very well in security litigation. While the circumstances of this particular incident, as tragic as it was, will likely not give rise to any litigation involving our company, the fact that we never took the time to ask about the nature and character of the property would likely not put us in the best light professionally, even though it may not harm us legally. There is currently a great amount of discussion in our industry concerning the standards for security officers, but one area of great concern is standards for the very services that we provide.

Many security practitioners do not know where to begin the process that will lead to making practical security recommendations to a prospective or current customer. Many do not think it is worth the effort when there is a low likelihood that they will be followed. While others may feel that it places the customer, and potentially the security company, in a precarious position if the recommendations are not acted upon. These are the primary reasons why most companies rely on the customer to dictate the hours, locations, and duties of the security officers. I have even seen the act of conducting a risk assessment for a potential customer, labeled as "supplemental" or "value-added" services. This almost seems to suggest that the act of conducting a risk assessment is only necessary if the customer is purchasing a premium service package; otherwise they just expect the new company to do exactly as the last company did. I have been told countless times that customers have no desire or interest in recommendations from the security company, since it memorializes in a document the deficiencies and vulnerabilities at the property. While there is always a danger of the material being discoverable (see Chapter 5 for more information), it has been my experience that most customers are eager to draw upon the experience and expertise of security practitioners. The willing acceptance, or the reluctance, of entering into a discussion concerning a comprehensive risk assessment often times is a reflection of how the subject is broached and what standards are being used. And as with any other profession, the average security services customer is interested in what everyone else is doing.

While the industry as a whole, and practitioners individually, sometimes struggle with benchmarks in the areas of security officer duties and competencies, there has been a lot of great work done in the area of standardizing basic risk assessment formulas. Each and every contract for security service should start out with the basic risk assessment being offered, and hopefully ultimately performed. Each customer and individual property present unique and different environments for potential security operations, but some common elements can be used in the risk assessment process. The following are the basic steps to the risk assessment process outlined in the ASIS International general security risk assessment guidelines.[3]

UNDERSTAND THE ORGANIZATION AND IDENTIFY THE PEOPLE AND ASSETS AT RISK

There is no one-size-fits-all approach to risk assessments. I will not commence a risk assessment until I have had a chance to speak in detail with the organization I am assessing. While there are standard assets inherent in any business, there will also be unique aspects depending on the environment. People and property are going to be a standard asset at every location. Every organization has a vested interest in keeping its employees and visitors safe, and depending on the nature of the business, more or less assets could be present. Personality of the business, standing in the community, and the reputation of the organization are often overlooked assets. Without knowing what is important to the customer, it is nearly impossible to know what their security needs are. For example, in healthcare settings patient satisfaction is the key. While this does not negate the need for effective access control and other security measures, without taking this philosophy into consideration some recommendations may make sense in the security context, but

---

[3]As of this writing, ASIS International is in the publication phase of the Risk Assessment ANSI Standard.

are impracticable because they don't line up with the organization's overall mission of serving the needs of patients and families.

A retail customer once asked me to speak to a gathering of local business owners at a shopping mall. It was just prior to the Christmas holidays and I had gone over a few helpful hints on how to recognize shoplifters and how to be aware of suspicious persons. At the conclusion of my presentation, one of the business owners asked the question "why can't we just keep all of the bad people out of the mall," thereby ensuring that no theft or other negative incidents would happen. Sounds simple enough, right? The obvious flaw in his question was that he was proposing to do the exact opposite of what he is in the business of encouraging: having people enter his business. I responded, trying to keep all the sarcasm in check, that this task was not only difficult to achieve, since there is no real formula or common sense criteria that could be employed to keep certain people out, unless they had a history with the mall or the security officers were trained in behavioral recognition, and the "bad" people showed warnings that would indicate an intent to commit crimes. But the real point was that effectively shutting down access would have potentially very negative consequences for the shopping mall in general and the businesses located within it specifically. Some properties may have the luxury of having very tight access control, while some depend on a free-flowing stream of customer traffic to survive. I have also been asked a variation at this question when conducting training for churches, casinos, and even restaurants. While the concern may be genuine, it is often up to the security practitioner to point out to the customer that there must be a balance of security and commerce, with both goals hopefully being ultimately achieved.

Just as the personality, philosophy, and mission of the organization must be clearly understood, the financial limitations must also be taken into account. Let me be clear: I have never hesitated to recommend a reasonable and necessary security measure to a customer because of some perceived lack of resources. But the keywords are *reasonable* and *necessary*. As with any profession, there is sometimes a tendency to overstate the importance of a potential service or a solution to an identified problem. I have always found it quite interesting how some organizations can go from one extreme to the other in the wake of a serious incident. Even more perplexing, is how the same organization will eventually revert back to the same, or in some cases even less, security measures than they had prior to the incident. Obviously, increased attention is warranted in the wake of a security-related tragedy such as a high-profile shooting or a major breach, but sometimes measures are offered up and implemented with the hopes of being permanent only to be eliminated when the memory of the incident fades. Sometimes, as security practitioners, we are tempted to start with offering the most costly and involved recommendations possible. The rationale is rooted in logic. The thought process usually follows that if the tightest security possible is employed, then most security risks are eliminated. But the stark reality is that security budgets are finite and have to be managed in a real-world business environment.

I was recently having a casual conversation with a friend who is in the advertising business. The conversation was based around budgets for various line items such as marketing and security. He was bemoaning the fact that organizations are not always willing to invest the money needed to truly establish their brand and bring about tangible growth through his efforts. As we began to talk about the many different challenges facing businesses these days, and how budgets in all areas are proving that we are all facing the prospect of doing more with less, he remarked "but I'm sure you never experience budget crunches since corporations and small businesses don't pinch pennies when it comes to security." After I realized that the statement was not made in jest, I explained to him the dollars spent on security are not vastly different than the dollars spent on any other business expense. They have never been unlimited, and they never will be. While one could debate the importance of security over other line items, the simple reality is that businesses in today's climate are forced to be as efficient and resourceful as possible. Without diluting our professional security opinions, recommendations, and meaningful guidance, this fact cannot be ignored. While a cost–benefit analysis is always an integral part of a sound security risk assessment, I prefer to have, at minimum, a cursory conversation concerning resources when I am evaluating the personality and character of the organization. Knowing what they can, will, and intend to do in the way of resources can be valuable information as you set upon the course of creating and providing a thoughtful risk assessment.

IDENTIFY VULNERABILITIES

Identifying the vulnerabilities at a certain location follows closely behind understanding the organization's personality and philosophy. A key concept in performing risk assessments is knowing what incidents are likely to occur at the property, and how frequently they may occur. While there are some common factors inherent in every facility such as external and internal theft, vandalism, and other various security breaches, the likelihood of such incidents can vary widely from industry to industry and from location to location. One of the greatest sources of this type of information is the customer themselves. Knowing what has transpired in the past can give a keen sense of what may transpire in the future. However, I have found that oftentimes customers are reluctant to share this information for a number of reasons. Since we are talking about legalities in the area of private security, one of the lessons that I have learned the hard way involves engaging the customer on what impact risk assessments may have on current or future litigation. After completing a somewhat brief risk assessment for a large hospital I found this out in a very abrupt way.

As I was traveling to the hospital, for my meeting with the executive staff where I intended to go through an exhaustive presentation on my evaluation of their current security measures and offer future recommendations, I received a rather frantic phone call from my customer contact. With a somewhat panicked tone he asked me if my presentation, and more importantly my written report, would include any reference to past security issues and vulnerabilities that had not been addressed. Since he had just outlined 90% of what was included in my presentation and report, I had no choice but to respond that it did include all of those elements. He then quickly advised me that I would need to omit any reference to past security vulnerabilities and incidents from both my written report and oral presentation. As I explained to him that my presentation would now basically consist of an introduction followed by a 5-min talk on a very generic and hypothetical set of healthcare circumstances, I advised that it may be best to postpone the meeting and talk further about the mission of the assessment. Only then did I learn that there were some very real and genuine concerns that my activities may give rise to discoverable material in any current or future lawsuits. This is a very real fear for many security practitioners and customers alike. Living in the legal world, I am hypersensitive to those concerns as well. But the irony in these situations is that many organizations allow themselves to be so paralyzed by the fear of creating a record of their shortcomings that they fail to take proactive measures that possibly could avoid legal actions in the future.

Like any good problem, this issue can in most cases be easily addressed with effective communication. Depending on the legal experience and awareness of the customer, it is usually solved by advising them that they need to involve their inside and/or outside counsel in the process to ensure that all communications are given the proper legal privilege and hopefully shielded from any harmful purposes in present and future litigation. While this may complicate and will likely lengthen the process, I have found that it is a very necessary step to ensure that neither side is blindsided when the subpoenas start flying down the road.

In addition to fears over whether or not a risk assessment will become the star witness in the next lawsuit, some customers have to be put at ease with the process of identifying vulnerabilities and past incidents due to their desire to protect the overall perception of the organization. Just as I find when answering the question my doctor asks every year at my annual check up about my diet and exercise routine, there is always a tendency to paint the picture a little brighter than it actually is. We all like to think that we are doing all that we can in such an important and critical area as security. This is the main reason I am no longer shocked when I talk to employees of the organization and get a vastly different perception of the security environment than what was presented to me when talking to executive leadership. It's not that I have been intentionally misled, it is simply the fact that we all would like to think that we are creating a happy, productive, and safe environment, and many times employees will tell an outsider things that they would never share with their employer. Based on this perception, it is critical to gain comprehensive and detailed information on what the organization and property is at risk for. Just as it does me no good to convince my doctor that I am the picture of health, a risk assessment will not be effective if it is not based on comprehensive risk data that is obtained by asking the right questions.

Is their product desirable to those on the outside and inside? Each time I have done a risk assessment in a food processing or food storage facility, it doesn't take much study or extensive expertise for me to realize that this is a product that has a high risk of theft. Does the profile of the company, its core beliefs, or its political activities create additional vulnerabilities and threats? In teaching a risk assessment class recently, I used the well-known restaurant chain Chick-fil-A as an example of evolving vulnerabilities. While I have never provided any service directly to the organization, I have been to their corporate office on several occasions. If I had been asked to perform a risk assessment at this location in June 2012, I would've offered up my standard recommendations and observations that would be appropriate for a national brand whose nerve center is located in a nondescript area outside of Atlanta, Georgia. Access control, patrol, and other routine security measures certainly would be common elements, as they would be for any large corporate headquarters, and the threat analysis would likely not have been very unique. If I was asked to perform the same assessment in mid-July of that same year, the observations and recommendations would look vastly different. What changed? Simply put: everything.

When Dan Cathy, the CEO of Chick-fil-A waded into the national conversation about marriage equality, the security dynamics of his organization drastically changed in an instant. Almost overnight, the backlash from those who did not agree with his position intensified and both sides of the debate reacted with great passion and emotion. While it is unknown what real security threats or challenges they actually faced in the days following the controversy, or in the 3 years since, it is certainly reasonable to assume that additional measures would have been warranted. And while every situation you encounter will not have the national prominence or drama of the Chick-fil-A saga, this example clearly illustrates the need to know what each organization and property is potentially dealing with during a risk assessment. Knowing what an organization faces is the first step to offering practical and reasonable solutions.

Beyond customer provided information, it is also imperative that the assessor seeks and obtains information from other sources. Sometimes, appearances can be very misleading. By examining data such as neighborhood crime information, prior lawsuits involving the property or company, and standard economic factors of the surrounding community, one can start to develop a sense of what the organization and property is faced with. The presence of certain businesses or environments surrounding the property can impact the level of vulnerability as well. Once while performing a security risk assessment for a US Department of Defense contractor, I noticed that the vacant lot on the east side of the factory was being prepared for construction. After the tour of the facility, and after I had already mentally prepared many of my recommendations, I thought to ask the person guiding me on my tour what was planned for the location. As he described to me the new privately owned residential complex that was being constructed in order to cater exclusively to college students attending a University several miles away, my focus somewhat shifted. The fence line that was in some disrepair and covered in vegetation had now become much more of an issue as I imagined several alcohol-fueled spontaneous field trips to the weapons factory next door.

In addition to common criminal threats, the assessor must also be careful not to overlook other scenarios that may pose potential risks to the property. Some organizations have given little thought to situations such as natural disasters, labor disputes, and other incidents that could result in the mission of the organization being interrupted. Business continuity and disaster recovery now play a prominent role in risk assessments. While criminal activity is a valid concern for any organization, natural disasters have the potential to cause even more disruption and damage. In today's business environment, we are all dependent on technology. As I write this, I have just experienced a very severe storm that resulted in a loss of power and communications for almost 72 hours at our corporate headquarters, and in other parts of the city it was even worse. While we have adequate back-up systems and redundancies in critical areas, we realized quickly that we are dependent on those who are supplying those services. Even after spending many hours crafting what we thought was an effective disaster recovery plan, we are now making several changes based on the recent lessons learned.

One blind spot in this area for customers who utilize security officer services is the impact that natural disasters will have on the existing security force. More often than not. the staff who is employed at the site will experience the same common struggles related to housing, transportation, and utilities interruption as the customer's direct employee population. This critical element oftentimes goes unrealized until the disaster hits and no personnel are available to staff the posts. Issues such as state-level industry regulations, and the lack of reciprocity among them, can further complicate matters when attempting to bring in officers from other areas. These issues, and related planning items such fuel, housing, and meals, should be addressed and itemized during an assessment, if an updated plan is not present.

PROBABILITY OF LOSS/FORESEEABILITY

Upon identifying the common and unique risks posed in the subject environment, the next logical step is to determine the likelihood of occurrence. Common risk threads such as outside criminal elements and internal losses may be standard for each property, but the chance of routine occurrences will vary widely by location and other factors. In this step, prior incidents play a key role. In drawing an accurate picture of the threats posed to a certain environment, it is important to acquire accurate and timely data. Being as specific as possible, when describing potential events is also essential, as it will radically change the perception of the customer and improve the process of acceptance. I have seen several assessment reports that note a high rate of criminal activity in the surrounding area, only to learn that most of the "activity" involved low-level traffic offenses or other minor infractions.

Gathering this data can be accomplished from several different sources. As previously described, the customer themselves can be a valuable tool for information concerning types of events and their frequency. Occasionally, you will encounter an organization, especially hospitals and educational intuitions, that keeps detailed internal records of incidents by type, location, and frequency. This can be a solid foundation when developing the probability of future losses. Local police departments are also available to provide area crime analysis for a specified area and time period. Law enforcement can also be a valuable source of intelligence concerning what has happened in the past, at a particular location.

Going beyond crime data, an assessor can gain valuable insight into the probability of loss for a property by looking at internal complaints or incidents that were never reported to law enforcement. Has the organization received any complaints from employees or visitors that can shed light on how frequently losses may occur? Are there any issues in the immediate neighborhood that could raise the level of risk for surrounding properties? These are all good questions to ask to get a keen insight into how likely certain things are to occur. This concept of determining the probability of events also brings to the forefront a very important and sometimes troubling concept for security companies: *Foreseeability*.

In litigation claiming some type of negligence on the part of the customer or the security company, the issue of foreseeability is front and center. There is no doubt that the measures employed to make the property secure will be second guessed by a plaintiff, who is seeking to recover because of a security-related incident. If the event was foreseeable, then there is now a hurdle that the defendant has to get over. Simply put, foreseeability is established by proof that a reasonable person of ordinary intelligence and circumspection, should reasonably have foreseen that his or her negligent act would imperil others. The question during litigation that will be addressed over and over is: Did you do enough? Were the security measures that were ultimately implemented adequate to protect the plaintiff from the harm he or she suffered? If you have the misfortune of being a defendant in a case that survives all the way to the trial stage, you will likely hear this theme as a centerpiece of the plaintiff's case. "If only ABC Security Company had done more," "if only the customer had paid for more officers," "if only the lighting had been a little better, my client would not be sitting here today dealing with the aftermath of their negligence." I have heard a version of this argument countless times, and it all comes down to foreseeability. Knowing what we know now, are we taking reasonable steps to secure this property? The answer could potentially have huge legal consequences down the road.

THE IMPACT OF LOSS EVENTS

I've always said that each and every business in existence is going to suffer some type of loss event in their history. Whether it is widespread industrial espionage that causes millions of dollars of damage to the valuation of the company, or a minor act of vandalism in a parking area, something will eventually occur. Part of a good risk assessment will involve determining what impact identified vulnerabilities will have on an organization. This is essential when it comes to mitigating threats, stopping events from occurring, and allocating finite resources to the proper areas.

While it is always ultimately the prerogative of the customer where they eventually expend resources and implement procedures, it is the responsibility of the assessor to highlight which areas are most critical and which areas are not. Several years ago, while performing a risk assessment for an educational institution I had begun the process of talking to several different staff members who worked in one of the academic buildings. Overall, the institution had several different security issues that needed to be addressed immediately and had recently experienced a tragic event on their campus that attracted a certain amount of negative public attention. Upon interviewing several employees, I noticed that a common theme was their concern over key control of a certain utility closet. Quite a bit of time was taken up discussing the frustration level of how several of the custodial employees would access the utility closet and fail to relock it when they were finished. There were even some who alleged that other employees from other departments within the University had been given keys to the utility closet without proper authorization. While it did not appear they had suffered any loss as of yet, it was very apparent to me that this was of great concern.

When I asked to be shown this utility closet, I was escorted to a small storage area that contained three mop buckets, a couple of brooms, and a handful of cleaning supplies. I've always been a proponent of the law enforcement and security approach known as the "Broken Windows" theory, which dictates that holding the line on small infractions will result in a greater overall sense of order thereby creating a safer environment. But sometimes an organization can lose focus, and it is up to the assessor to gently guide them back to the big picture. While certainly not diminishing the need to stop any type of unauthorized access to all areas, and I'm sure I could've constructed several different scenarios as to how unfettered access to this particular storage area could have resulted in greater harm down the road, I had to quickly note that the impact of a staff member accessing this closet would be very minimal financially and otherwise. This is often a delicate balance, but determining the impact a loss event can have on organization is critical when it comes to suggesting certain measures.

I ask most customers at the inception of an assessment what their greatest assets are and what critical areas they are most dependent upon. The most obvious response for any organization is its people. As security providers, our number one goal is to protect the employees and visitors from any harm. Measures such as sound-access control, adequate security in parking areas, and having an effective workplace violence and active shooter response plan are the necessary elements for any security program. Beyond that, each organization will have unique and varied needs when it comes to determining what loss event might have the most severe impact. While every organization in modern times is to some degree dependent upon technology for communication and for delivering their products and services, some industries such as banking may suffer a greater casualty due to the loss of Internet service. Without a proper inquiry, it is often hard to surmise what critical components need to be the most secure and safeguarded from outside threats. Backup systems and recovery time should also be discussed and addressed during this phase. In the past several years, disaster recovery and business continuity have become hallmarks of any well-thought-out assessment process. It is never been more critical to ensure that operations can function at all times, even in the midst of a man-made or natural disaster.

RECOMMENDATIONS TO MITIGATE RISK

Offering practical and reasonable recommendations to counteract the identified risks is the element in the assessment process that will attract the most discussion and attention. In conjunction with looking at resources that are required to implement the solution, the impact of mitigation measures on business flow and the overall operation are also the key points to be discussed by all stakeholders. This is an evolutionary process. Mitigation measures can, and in most cases should, change over time depending on the evolving threats and business needs. Mitigation measures should be recommended while keeping in mind the organization's overall mission, resources, and the likelihood of effectively addressing the vulnerability in question. This can be a tall order, and balancing all interests can require a thorough examination of the pros and cons of each measure. I have had several customers tell me that they want their facility to be as secure as it possibly can be. While the intent of the statement is well understood and is offered as a way to convey an overall commitment to doing whatever it takes to protect the people and assets, the reality is that commerce and security have to coexist.

Recent headlines never disappoint when I'm looking for an example to illustrate how difficult it can be to construct a scenario in which a facility is 100% secure from any outside threats or breaches. The White House is arguably the most secure place of business in the country, if not the world. The average citizen would assume that there are measures in place that would prevent any act of aggression against the property, or at minimum stop any attempt of unauthorized access. And while there are layers upon layers of physical security in and around the complex, we've also seen that nothing is totally foolproof.

I'm sure that many Americans were shocked at the images that emerged in September 2014, of an individual running across the North lawn of the White House, successfully entering an exterior door, and eventually briefly stepping in to the East room. This caused many to question, and rightfully so, how such a serious breach could occur. While the actual events and security deficiencies have been widely reported on, and there is no doubt in my mind that the measures that were already in place were not adequately followed or implemented, I believe that the response to this incident, and others like it, represents a good example of an organization attempting to manage public image and security.

In 1995, the decision was made to close Pennsylvania Avenue in front of the White House. This step was taken mainly in response to the Oklahoma City bombing tragedy and other world events that had given the Secret Service a reason for concern. While I scarcely remember the days when tourists were free to drive up and down this two block stretch hoping to catch a glimpse of the current occupant, I do recall a fair amount of public reaction to this measure. Some saw this as one more step toward total isolation of the "people's house," and part of the evolution toward making it into a fortified compound that would ultimately bear no resemblance to a public place. In the wake of the latest fence jumper incident, the Secret Service announced the plan to enhance the security of the fence by adding angled spikes at the top. As the spokesperson commented, this should bring the incidence of fence jumping down to an "acceptable level."[4] Acceptable level? Wouldn't an acceptable level be zero? Not necessarily.

Could more be done to prevent fence jumping at the White House? Absolutely! For starters, a complete shutdown of Pennsylvania Avenue to pedestrian traffic and sealing off the surrounding perimeter to anyone not authorized to be there would be a great first step. Beyond that, installing more secure and higher fencing around the entire property would serve further to deter, or at least sufficiently delay, someone wishing to breach the property. The problem? This would of course do serious harm to the aesthetics of one of our most prized and cherished landmarks, and would also send a potentially troubling message to the citizens who own the property. In the world of security, the theoretical "best" does not always equal reality "best."

It is unlikely that you will face a set of facts with national and global implications such as White House security, but the concerns are just as real when dealing with your customer. The measures recommended have to be seen through the prism of public image, business necessities, and maintaining security. At the conclusion of conducting an assessment at another large educational institution, I was asked to prepare a proposal and a detailed implementation plan for placing metal detectors at each entrance to the college. College leadership was concerned about recent events at other campuses and wanted to ensure that all possible steps were being taken to

[4]White House Fence Security Breach. http://www.politico.com/story/2015/05/white-house-fence-security-breach-secret-service-117732.html

prevent violence on their campus. While it was hard to argue that measures such as screening every single student, faculty member, and visitor would not result in mitigating the risk of weapons on campus, it was time to turn the discussion to other implications that may have resulted from the decision. How would implementing metal detectors at every door, aside from the logistical issues of doing so with such a large campus, impact the overall perception and public image of the school? How would it affect the flow of classroom instruction day-to-day? Screening hundreds of students, going from one building to the other, each day would have had major implications and would likely radically change the student environment. These are the questions that needed to be answered, and can only be truly answered by the leadership who bore that responsibility. At the end of the day it is the assessor's job to point out these concerns, but the customer's job is to decide what direction to go in.

It is always a best practice to directly link the recommended mitigating measure to the actual vulnerability identified. This will serve you well in the event of security litigation. In addition to identifying a mitigating measure, a thorough explanation of how the process works and what the desired result will be should be included as well. Without clear guidance and instructions, the implementations of mitigation measures often fail. I've seen this countless times in the area of access control. The primary focus of access control is to let the right people in and keep the wrong people out; it is a very basic and easily understood principle. However, I have seen several situations where physical security measures are put in place but no real criteria is developed to govern how they are used. This is extremely common in the residential services area.

Many gated complexes or communities have the appearance of adequate physical controls, but there is no clear criterion as to who is allowed on the property and who is not. This conflict will inevitably rear its head if litigation is commenced. While working on a recent case, I discovered that the complex in question had state-of-the-art physical security controls, security officer presence, and many other security aspects to potentially guard the tenants from outside criminal activity. The problem? In spite of all these great tools, anyone could walk up or drive up and be allowed immediate access, regardless of whether or not they were a tenant or legitimately visiting someone who was. Were the security measures adequate and reasonable? Because there was no method to enforce their intent, that question will likely be a hotly debated topic during this case.

The most important aspect of any assessment, and the bottom line when it comes to setting yourself up to be in the best position possible when litigation arises, is to ensure that all the vulnerabilities are identified and reasonable measures are offered as a way to mitigate them. And while it does not mean that failure is certain in a court of law if all measures are not embraced totally and quickly implemented, a thorough assessment and documented evaluation process will put you, and possibly your customer, in the best light possible. Conducting steps such as cost–benefit analysis, feasibility studies, and other components of the assessment process will show that you are thorough and had the genuine goal of achieving the safest property possible. The information that you gather and the recommendations that you make, are also essential ingredients to developing operating procedures for the security staff.

OPERATING PROCEDURES

Operating procedures, often called post instructions or post orders, play an extremely vital role in security litigation. The key question in most security negligence cases is did you do enough to prevent what happened? But before we usually get to that point, we have to ask what were we actually supposed to do? Any time an incident lands on my desk one of the first things I request is the operating procedures at that location. I then begin to investigate whether or not these instructions were being followed before, during, and after the event in question. I have often said that post operating procedures can be an attorney's best friend, or most vicious enemy in security litigation. If the post orders are reasonably and thoughtfully constructed to address known issues at the property, and the security officer has followed the instructions, we are at a good starting point for a defense. But if the operating procedures are outdated, irrelevant, or are not being followed on a consistent basis, the ride just got a little more rocky. I have seen many situations where boilerplate post instructions were offered in place of specific guidelines for the property in question. Trying to explain why there were instructions present that bear no real relevance and were not applicable to any present issues at the property, can make for a long day of testimony. And occasionally minor wording in the instructions can take on a larger meaning.

A peaceful morning approximately 2 years ago was interrupted by a phone call informing me that we were now a defendant in a lawsuit concerning a workplace shooting. The shooting had occurred a year earlier and involved an employee, who worked at a large industrial complex, being shot multiple times by a fellow employee. Miraculously, the shooting victim had survived but was suffering with severe physical effects and would need continual care throughout his life. The Workmen's Compensation case between the victim and our customer had concluded, and now he was attempting to recover from us based on the theory of negligent security. One rule I have attempted to live by in my legal career is to never underestimate any situation where we are a named defendant in a lawsuit, and I always try to avoid adopting the attitude of being nonchalant or dismissive just because I know the "real facts." I pride myself on approaching every situation with the same level of diligence and respect for the process. I have learned many times that the one action that appears to have no chance of succeeding may be the very one that does. But on this day, I did venture into "there is nothing we could of done different" territory. After talking to the management employees involved in the situation, and even having a discussion with our customer representative, I felt very confident that we had provided competent services and this was to be just one of those situations, as tragic as the result was, where not much more could have been done to prevent it.

The post instructions were clear: officer must visibly check all employee ID badges before allowing entrance onto the property. It was undisputed that the shooter in this case was a current employee with a valid employee ID. He was not an intruder, or someone who had successfully breached security in order to exact revenge or punishment on this employee. He had every right to be there. Based on witness statements, there was no indication, when the shooter arrived for work that day, that he was agitated or upset, and he did not exhibit any type of threatening behavior when coming through the employee entrance. Short of conducting a full personal search of each employee entering the gate every morning or implementing metal detectors at the employee entrance, there was not much more that could have been offered to prevent this criminal act. In addition, each shift involves over 200 employees coming and going rendering personal screening nearly impossible and impractical. However, I knew from the outset that the plaintiff would likely offer the addition of these measures as proof that more could have been done to prevent the tragedy. And while this argument was repeatedly made, and I was prepared to refute it based on the fact that the measures would not have been reasonable for a variety of reasons, I quickly learned that another angle would cause me problems.

When I first visited the site after the shooting, my attention was immediately drawn to the sign posted by the employee entrance: *No Weapons Allowed Inside the Facility*. This is a sign that I've seen dozens of times before in a variety of different environments to communicate to employees and visitors alike that weapons are not allowed. My initial reaction as I snapped several pictures of the sign was that it was an excellent visual to show that the shooter had obviously been on notice that weapons were not allowed inside the facility and he willingly violated the rule. No doubt he was really the one responsible. But as with any other case like this one, the shooter now resided in a correctional facility, and I was fairly certain he did not carry a large general liability policy that would satisfy the victim's damages. So it all came down to us.

As I prepared to be deposed, I went through my routine of reviewing all the contractual documents, police reports, witness statements, personnel files, and of course the post instructions. When reviewing the operating procedures, I did not see anything alarming or unusual, and I felt very confident that the measures we had in place had resulted in a reasonable and adequate security program. After enduring the standard questions about hiring, training, and who decided what the guard hours and duties would be, the plaintiff's attorney quickly turned to the post instructions. I began to be led down a road I had traveled many times before. "Mr Sorrells these operating procedures are what governed the security officers duties and responsibilities correct?" After a couple of more questions to make sure I was on the record emphasizing the critical importance of the post instructions he was holding in his hand, I knew that the counterpunch would be highlighting something in the instructions that we did not do. While this is a routine technique in security litigation depositions, and one that I had surely anticipated in this particular case, I had not prepared for what he had planned next. "Mr Sorrells, please read the third line from the top of the second page of the post operating procedures". I looked down and saw the words that I had reviewed previously: *security officers will strictly enforce all safety and security rules established and issued by the customer.* A rather benign statement that is included in virtually every set of post orders in existence. But my sense of calm went slightly off track when the next item I was handed was a photograph of the "no weapons" sign that I had been certain would work in our favor.

After some back and forth about how the "no weapons" sign could or could not be classified as within the meaning of the rules that we were being asked to enforce, I was ultimately in a position to address what steps were being taken to enforce this rule. While to this day I do not believe that it impacted the liability aspect of this case, it did remind me of how powerful written post operating procedures can be in security litigation. They will ultimately govern what you're being asked to do, and what you eventually did, to prevent bad acts. In the hands of a skilled plaintiff's attorney, or even an average one, many areas of post instructions can be exploited and used to get one step closer to proving negligence. The process of developing them should not be taken lightly. While some stock language may be appropriate from site to site, specificity is critical to avoid liability.

Many operating procedures use generic phrases such as "officer will control access to the premises," rather than detailing what those access control procedures are. How is he or she supposed to address the visitors? Are they being asked to control access, but the post instructions also require them to be in other areas performing tasks such as patrol? Is this practical, or even humanly possible? I have also seen very broad language concerning how frequently and in what areas, the security officer should be present. Since one of the central questions will be "where was the officer located when this happened?," having at least some sense of chronology in the post instructions would be helpful. One of the most overlooked aspects of post instructions is documenting the receipt of the instructions by the officer, and some demonstration of competency in order to neutralize any questions about whether or not the security officers had adequate knowledge to perform the task. In addition to this, it is also advisable to have some communication and/or documentation between the security company and the customer showing agreement with the post instructions. This will hopefully eliminate any back-and-forth pertaining to which party actually knew and approved of what the duties and responsibilities were.

So back to the question at hand; who is the decider? The answer is simple. It always has been and always will be the customer. But in order to make the final decision they must have adequate information and guidance from industry professionals. Never accept the *status quo* or get sucked into playing the game of "here are the post orders from the last company." Always be prepared to view each individual site as unique in its strengths and weaknesses because it is. You may eventually find yourself implementing the *status quo*, but make certain that it is after a deliberate and thorough process that will be the building block to a successful defense when litigation comes. And as we will see, the steps you take at this early stage will impact you in many different ways as you travel the road to the courthouse door.

Chapter 3

Sign here please: rules of legal engagement

"Let's seal the deal with a handshake." How long has it been since you have heard that proposed as a way to finalize a contractual arrangement? I would bet even if you have heard it recently, it did not ultimately work out to be literally true. Unfortunately or fortunately, depending on which side of the table you are sitting on, business of any nature is rarely transacted without the necessity of some type of written agreement outlining the parties' responsibilities to one another, compensation, insurance requirements, and other legal ground rules for the relationship.

Whether we realize it or not, each of us enters into some type of contract each day. How many times in the past week have you visited a website to download a song, or to perform some type of basic search? Before proceeding you were likely asked to acknowledge certain terms and conditions that each and every one of us blindly do without reading as much as a sentence. We do so because we have no choice if we want to purchase the goods or services, and because the terms are not offered as an option to consider. These are known in the legal world as contracts of adhesion. In these situations the consumer has little or no bargaining power in regard to the terms and conditions that are being agreed to, and it truly is a "take it or leave it" scenario. While courts do occasionally scrutinize these types of agreements, and have been known to invalidate ones that are held to be unconscionable, for the most part they are perfectly legal. We are taught in law school that contracts are typically only enforceable when there has been some type of bargaining and mutual assent to the agreed upon terms. But in these scenarios that doesn't always hold true. The next time you book a hotel room for the night, purchase a song on iTunes, or sign up for cell phone service, let the other party know that you wish to modify certain terms on the standard contract or legal notice. I'll save you some time. If you refuse to agree, you don't get the room, you won't hear the song, and you'll have no way to call and complain to someone about it. Does this one-sided approach rear its head in our industry? It certainly can.

I have seen some agreements that consist of just a few paragraphs, but I have also encountered contracts that bear a striking resemblance to a paperback novel with dozens of pages of clauses and attachments that take hours to examine and analyze. The simple reality is that the contractual process has become more difficult and cumbersome over the last several years. The reason: lawsuits. Each party now attempts to cover any and all legal blind spots that have the potential for causing them financial harm in the future. And on occasion, new contractual theories are created to deal with recent experiences. I have seen the process evolve over the last two decades into a fairly one-sided scenario where the service provider is sometimes forced to choose between the business and the comfort of legal protections. While it is increasingly difficult to achieve, a situation where you can obtain both is ideal.

Before we get into the art of constructing the actual agreement, we must first acknowledge the reality of contract negotiations in the security services industry. One of the critical lessons that eluded me in my law school career was the fact that the art of negotiation is just as important, if not more so, than what actually goes into the agreement. The offering of security services is a somewhat unique situation where the customer often dominates the contracting process. Consider for a moment what reaction you would get if you decided to purchase a new vehicle, but decided to make your own rules. You select the make and model you want to purchase and make the trip to your local dealership. You greet the salesperson and deliver the good news that there will be no need for high-pressure tactics or attractive offers of "complementary" services to seal the deal; you have already made up your mind that you want the car and are willing to pay full sticker price. All that remains is to memorialize the deal with a sales contract. Imagine if at that pivotal moment you reach into your briefcase and announce that as the customer you have drafted your own legal agreement and you expect the dealership to execute it with little or no modifications. Furthermore, you will be forgoing the act of signing anything drafted by the dealer or the car manufacturer. After questions concerning whether or not you even possess the mental capacity to enter into a valid contract, I would guess that you would not be driving off the lot in a shiny new car when the dust settles. This scenario sounds illogical and anyone that attempted it would be deemed at best unreasonable, but that is what happens each day in the security services contracting process. The customer is often in control.

Several years ago, I received a phone call from one of our sales representatives who had some exciting news. After many years of courting, he had finally landed a potential deal with one of the largest and most recognizable corporations in the world. If everything worked out, we could stand to gain a sizable contract that would hopefully result in a long and prosperous relationship for both parties. He explained to me that they were at the stage of sending us a national contract for review and I should be receiving it any day. Several days later I received a rather voluminous package and began to pour over dozens of pages of agreements, accompanied by numerous exhibits and attachments, concerning issues such as insurance requirements, safety standards, and hold harmless agreements. During my review I noted several areas of the agreement that were not only troubling, but could even leave us exposed without insurance coverage in certain situations. I also found that many provisions were extremely one-sided and would operate to shift virtually all liability to our company, even for acts that bore no real connection to our services. I carefully cataloged each area and drafted alternative language for each. My proposed substitutes were not unreasonable, and truth be known, would still result in the liability scales tipping in their favor, should any type of loss occur. I then contacted my counterpart who represented our prospective customer and set up a time to discuss my concerns and hopefully reach a compromise.

At the appointed time, I reached out to my contact to discuss drafting an agreement we could both live with. After some small talk about our respective industries and companies, I began to outline some of my concerns and communicated my willingness to do whatever possible to reach a middle ground that would allow us to move forward with the deal. At the conclusion of my brief presentation, the answer came very quickly; leaving no doubt about the next step. "Eddie, I want to apologize for not making this clear sooner, but we will not change a word of the agreement." "It is basically a take it or leave it proposition." "If you want to do business with us, it must be signed without any modifications, whatsoever." After some additional discussions about how there were a dozen other companies who were vying for the same contract that would be willing to sign the agreement on a moment's notice, any hope for reaching middle ground was a distant memory. So much for meaningful negotiations.

I am sure that many legal and management professionals in our industry can relate similar stories, and that same scenario has played out many times in my career since that meeting. While it is unfortunate, it is also a fact of business life that will likely never change. I don't want to suggest that all customers take this rigid uncompromising position when it comes to contract negotiations, as I have also had the contrasting experience of sitting down with parties who are more than willing to make certain concessions after listening to a reasoned explanation as to why it would be detrimental to our company. But in the same way that a car dealership is prohibited from deviating, from their standard agreement because of the various laws and regulations they have to meet when transacting with a customer, the purchasers of our services have certain obligations they feel have to be met. The attorneys, purchasing agents, and management contacts who we deal with, are tasked with making sure that they are protected from any adverse circumstances that may arise in connection with our services. The best way to do this is to draft an ironclad agreement that does not allow for any deviations. Just as service providers must evaluate what type of customer environment poses the most risks, our customers must also evaluate what written agreements have the potential for putting them in legal peril, when losses occur for reasons connected to our services.

At best, this is a delicate balance between securing the business and shielding the company legally from any unnecessary and unintended liability. I have been asked before to draft a contract that would virtually guarantee that all liability would be eliminated, or at a minimum, severely limited. Without digging into the minutia of state-by-state laws concerning contract enforcement, it is reasonable to assume that one could create a contract that is drafted with the sole intent of shifting nearly all liability to the other party. And unfortunately, I have been on the wrong end of that scenario in the past. This is where the intersection of the lawyer and the businessperson truly rises to the surface. What good is a carefully crafted contract that serves as an effective way to bar most successful legal actions in the future, if no one will agree to sign it?

In the aftermath of the Virginia Tech shooting in 2007, many in our industry were concerned about what legal implications may arise for security services providers, if or when, an active shooting takes place at a customer location. Just as would be the case with any other crime that occurs on customer property, the security company will always be a likely civil defendant and will be forced to defend their actions, or lack thereof. One of the methods to combat this liability that had been discussed in some insurance circles, was to add certain contractual language into standard security services agreements that sought to disclaim any liability on behalf of the security services provider and immunize them from future suits, resulting from workplace shootings. The intent was genuine, and I fault no one for attempting to better serve their insureds by coming up with methods to shield them from legal actions, where there may be any genuine legal liability, but an uphill climb to a viable defense. So I did not see anything inherently wrong, or professionally out of bounds, when I received an email in late 2007 from a colleague in the insurance industry seeking to address this important topic.

The email explained that due to the recent increase of active shootings at educational institutions and other various workplace environments, security companies were being urged to adopt new and improved language in their standard service agreements to disclaim any guarantees that its services will prevent such occurrences or the damages that necessarily flow from the same. There was even a suggested model clause to this effect.

Security Company undertakes no liability, or any form of legal responsibility, in connection with the prevention of, detection of, or response to any workplace shooting or related workplace violence. Its services are not designed or intended to prevent such occurrences and nothing contained in this agreement should be construed as a guarantee, expressed or implied, that such services will result in the prevention any such loss.

Seems to cover it pretty well, and I would be less than sincere if I suggested that I would not sleep better at night knowing that the clause was included in the hundreds of contracts that are lying dormant just waiting to be inserted into a legal battle. But the question often turns on business necessities and what the customer is willing to bargain for. Upon receiving this email, the question that I had to ask myself was this: is it a wise business decision to send each customer a new contract highlighting the need to disavow any responsibility related to active shooters? During this same time period, I was fielding many requests from our customers to consult on this very issue and provide training and guidance to assist them in their prevention efforts. Would this be the right time to disclaim any liability? While I have not seen this language, or any other like provision, tested in court, I decided that it was not in our best interest for long-term customer relations and retention to pursue this course.

There is no easy answer to these types of questions and each situation will be unique in its facts and circumstances. I am still looking for that elusive crystal ball that will give me definitive answers about which contracts are worth it and which ones are not, but I have learned that there is a formula that can put you in the best position possible.

An informed decision is a good decision. The key to successful contract negotiations and sound agreements is knowing exactly what your risks are and the potential consequences. This can only occur when you have a complete understanding of what the contract you are entering into really means. Some have adopted the approach of closing their eyes, holding their breath, and signing whatever is put before them, and hoping that things work out okay. And even though I have encountered many situations similar to the one I described about an unyielding customer prospect, I have also encountered several willing parties on the other side of the table, who will sign our agreement without as much as giving it a cursory review. This may work for some, and if you have ample resources and a forgiving insurance company, you may not encounter tremendous problems with this approach. But in most cases, not knowing what you are agreeing to, will likely come back to haunt you in the future.

So the first step in entering into the best contract possible is having as much information as you can. Many seemingly simple aspects of the proposed relationship can have a large impact on the contractual language. Several years ago, I began utilizing a contract information sheet that is submitted prior to the drafting or review of any agreement. This gives me the relevant information that I need to make sure all the bases are covered in our contract, or when reviewing the customer's proposed agreement.

The checklist is very simple but is a valuable tool in the precontracting process.

<u>CHECKLIST FOR CUSTOMER CONTRACTS</u>

<u>The following checklist must be completed for all new business and submitted along with contract for review.</u>

Contract Name: _____

Date Submitted: _____ Submitted by:_____

Bill Rate:_____ Pay Rate: _____

1. Is Company currently providing service for this customer?   YES   NO

   If yes, what date was service started: _____

   If no, what is the anticipated start date: _____

2. List amount of coverage under this contract: _____HPW (hours per week).

                ARMED   **UNARMED** (circle one)

3. Has customer provided Company with postorders or any other operating instructions?

YES   **NO**

    If yes, please attach a copy of orders.

4. Has a security assessment been performed and submitted to customer?

YES   **NO**

5. Will Officers be expected to drive customer-owned vehicles?   **YES** **NO**

6. Will Officers be expected to drive Company-owned vehicles?   **YES**   **NO**

7. Please list the following equipment that Company has agreed to provide to customer:

(e.g., tour system, radios, cell phones, computers, etc.)

_____

_____

_____

8. Please explain how the items in #7 are being billed (i.e., built into rate, etc.)

_____

_____

9. What State will this service be performed in? _____

10. What type of business is customer involved in? _____

Utilizing a checklist such as this, or any variation that gives essentially the same information, can greatly enhance the contracting process and make it much more efficient. Instead of spending time making numerous phone calls or sending emails requesting information, all of what I need to begin the review process is at my fingertips. Some information may not appear to be extremely important or relevant, but simple matters such as ownership of vehicles can radically alter certain contractual implications. Having a comprehensive understanding of all facts surrounding the potential business will serve you well in the process of contract construction, negotiation, and execution.

It is my experience that it is the exception rather than the rule that a security company will have readily available services of an in-house counsel to review all contracts, or draft an original agreement, when the need arises. Many use outside counsel for this purpose, but it may not always be practical economically, or fit in to the present time-table, to engage an attorney's services. In some situations, security company executives must make important determinations about the terms and conditions they are obligating themselves and the company too. This task can be monumental and quite overwhelming to someone not well-versed or experienced in legal matters and contract nuances. This can result in disaster when the true meaning of contracts only becomes evident after litigation is commenced. So let's look at the key steps and elements in the contract process from a layman's point of view, starting with different types of agreements and the pitfalls you are likely to encounter along the way. There are literally dozens of potential contractual issues and they could fill volumes with a full exposition of the current law on each. But the following is an examination of the most critical areas that come up in security services litigation.

YOUR STANDARD AGREEMENT[1]

There is a reason that every organization from doctors' offices to cell phone providers has their own contract. While it seeks to outline the terms and conditions of the customer relationship, it also primarily exists to protect the interests of the company providing the services. Any business relationship should be essentially a two-way street, and it is always in the security company's best interest to have a standard agreement that clearly establishes the responsibilities, terms, and obligations expected of both parties. Depending on how varied the customer base is, many companies also have differing standard agreements for different customer segments. For example, residential security services could be drafted with different provisions in the contract than those utilized in industrial settings. But regardless of how in-depth the company goes in the contracting process, a standard agreement should be a staple. We have already discussed some of the challenges in attempting to use a security services company generated agreement in lieu of a customer document. But those situations aside, the security company's agreement should be the default contract in all situations.

My standard practice is to at minimum communicate our desire to use our agreement and send the standard agreement for review by the other side. Even if utilizing our agreement is dismissed from the outset, and it often is, it can serve as a valuable reference point when negotiating specific clauses in the customer agreement. Many times while working with the other side in crafting compromising language, I have referred to sections and clauses in our agreement as a potential substitute. And while this does not happen in every situation, there have been some occasions where we have circled back to our original agreement, and with some modifications, it became the prevailing document. There are other situations where our standard agreement will become the baseline for a hybrid document that is produced by combining the best, and in some cases the worst, of both versions.

As with any other legal document, a standard services agreement needs to be drafted with great care and caution. It truly should be a multidisciplinary process. The obvious starting point would be an in-house counsel or trusted outside attorney, who would draft an initial version after a thorough understanding of the types of services offered. The next step would be to have your insurance carrier and claims management representatives review the document and make comments regarding appropriate revisions to the final draft. The inclusion of insurance professionals is key as they can interpret insurance requirements and related clauses in light of current coverage and

---

[1]A Sample Standard Security Services Agreement is included as Appendix A.

past claims. I have found that it's a good idea to keep any major surprises to a minimum, when it comes to filing insurance claims.

When you have successfully drafted a standard security services agreement, all company management and supervisory employees should be aware that this is in fact the approved method of contracting for your services. Some internal system should also be in place to seek and gain approval for any proposed modifications to the agreement. I've seen several instances, usually during the discovery phase of the trial, where an otherwise solid contract was marked through or modified in some way prior to execution because it seemed to be a minor point that needed to be clarified. Depending on the modification, this could throw an entire case in reverse headed for legal chaos.

On an annual basis, and certainly after every major lawsuit or liability event, the agreement should be reviewed for needed modifications. This should also involve a wide spectrum of professionals, including legal and insurance. Evaluating current case law, claims decisions, and your own internal experiences, you can gather valuable information on what needs to be added, changed, or taken out of your current agreement.

"BOILERPLATE" AGREEMENTS

Many organizations that purchase our services rely on standard agreements for a variety of different purposes. While not unheard of, most companies do not have a specific agreement for security services. This results in agreements being presented to the security company that may be completely devoid of any information or direction relating to our services. The only true modifications that are often made to these agreements are inserting the name of the security company and the date of execution. And to complicate matters further, these agreements are often drafted with other specific industries beside security in mind. I have reviewed hundreds of these agreements that are clearly created for the purpose of purchasing construction services and other types of general labor. They are littered with safety clauses, insurance language, and other verbiages that have no relevance to services performed by security officers. Many people would take the approach that since it is not relevant, there is no reason to be concerned about altering or removing the sections. In fact, when I have raised objections from time to time about using an alternative agreement, or at minimum redrafting the agreement to remove any reference to provisions that clearly don't apply, I have been met with the response of "don't worry, let's just sign it since we realize none of that will apply to your company." Sounds harmless enough, but how harmless is it to obligate yourself to something in writing that you clearly never intend to follow?

I have been faced with this question a number of times in depositions, and I can assure you that offering a response of "oh yes I knew the contract contained that language, but I was told not to worry about it since it did not apply," will likely paint you into a corner that is not very easy to get out of. At the hands of a reasonably skilled plaintiff's attorney, that one statement can make everything in the contract, and more troubling the company's credibility, suspect. The one-time I offered this as an explanation as to why a particular contract provision was not followed or enforced, I was quickly met with the textbook response, cleverly disguised as a question in search of an answer, of "how could anyone be certain that we followed any of our contractual obligations since it was obvious that we felt we had the right to pick and choose which applied and which did not." Make no mistake, the other side likely knew that was a function of boilerplate language that was not always applicable, but they did not hesitate to exploit it and call attention to the fact that obviously you "conduct your business in such a haphazard manner that you're not sure of what your true responsibilities are." And yes, that is an actual quote directed at me during one of the longest deposition days in recent memory.

When I find a party to be hesitant to reinvent the wheel and throw out a boilerplate agreement and start over, I offer to draft addendums to clarify certain provisions, our use the old-fashioned method of marking through and initialing things that do not apply. While this is not ideal, it does document your intent to clarify exactly what the roles and responsibilities were and what provisions actually applied to your services. And as we continue later on the journey of looking at relevant provisions, you'll see that this could have a major impact.

BATTLE OF THE FORMS[2]

A unique situation can arise when multiple agreements, or other additional forms, are utilized to govern the security services relationship. I have received an informal education in this area on multiple occasions. During my time as a law student, but already having several years of experience in the security services industry, I would routinely negotiate and secure contracts as part of my daily duties. I can recall one such occasion where I was tasked with getting an agreement executed with a rather large customer, who I

---

[2]The traditional meaning of this legal issue is rooted in the problem that arises when goods are routinely purchased with preprinted forms that are exchanged and have different terms. It is used here in the context of service agreements where dueling contracts are presented or other documents are used to establish terms and conditions. The battle is often "won" by the last party to present their agreement.

anticipated would not eagerly accept our standard agreement for execution. To my pleasant surprise, the process flowed very smoothly and resulted in a rather prompt signature on our standard agreement without modification. In the midst of patting myself on the back for doing such an admirable job of protecting our liability interests by having our agreement signed, my jubilation was interrupted by an email from my counterpart now asking me to sign their standard agreement. As I reviewed the attached document along with his instructions to sign as soon as possible and return it so we could "be set up for future payment," it did not take long to realize that everything contained in it was the legal polar opposite of our agreement that had just been executed. In fact, although I knew that it was logistically impossible, I temporarily allowed myself to consider the possibility that the agreement had been drafted for the sole purpose of nullifying the provisions in the document that was just executed. But as I have learned many times since that first occasion, this is a routine process that many customers employ when contracting for services. And to answer the question you're probably asking yourself, yes I signed the second agreement.

Fortunately I never faced an incident or situation that would have forced me to examine the impact of having dueling agreements, but this raises an interesting legal situation known as the "battle of the forms." The dilemma of both parties presenting contracts with differing terms goes back many years and is most often seen when parties utilize purchase orders (POs) for the sale of goods. For over 100 years, courts have struggled with what to do when both the parties present boiler-plate forms that were in conflict. The old common-law mirror image theory held that if one party presented contractual terms that differed from the original presentment from the other party, then the contract would be null and void since there was no mutual acceptance of the terms. However, under the "last shot rule", the party deemed to have presented their terms and conditions at the final stage of the process, and there was no objection to them by the other party, was usually seen as controlling the deal since they fired the last round prior to performance.

These antiquated legal concepts still echo throughout the contract process, but old common law theories have been avoided in many service contracts by inserting clauses that explicitly state that the agreement supersedes and replaces any prior agreement and leaves little doubt as to what governs the relationships. To complicate matters further, a familiar problem often rears its head in the process: *words*.

It is not unusual for a customer or prospect to present varying forms of documentation labeled in a variety of benign ways. "Contractor packet," "vendor qualification form," "business associate application," and "partner profile" are just a few of the labels that have seen to describe what is essentially a contract by any legal definition. To the lay manager, there can be no reason for hesitation prior to executing, what will later be realized is a full-blown legally binding contract. I have also had occasions where customer representatives will tell me that the document I am being asked to sign is in no way a contractual agreement but rather the required form that must be completed in order to set us up in the vendor payment system. While I have never suspected that this was due to any malicious intentions, the fact remains that this is often literally and legally incorrect. Regardless of what the heading suggest, or what the person on the other side is telling you, anything with terms and conditions that you're being asked to agree to, is a contract and your company can be held accountable for adhering to the responsibilities and obligations contained therein.

In our industry you will probably encounter this most often when dealing with the issue of POs. While rare, I have dealt with several situations where the customer has asked that there be no contract utilized by either party in order to avoid a formal budgeting process or other organizational hurdles they may encounter in their business procedures. While this is a somewhat odd request and can be concerning on a number of different levels, each time I have been confronted with this proposal, a small voice in the back of my head always asks the question "what's the catch"? Usually the catch is the PO that arrives shortly thereafter chock-full of terms and conditions concerning everything from hourly rates to hold harmless provisions. What happened to not having a contract? This can also complicate future discovery in lawsuits, and especially when trying to determine controlling indemnification provisions that may or may not be triggered. I have learned to use very broad wording beyond the stereotypical "contract", when asking our employees for documents to make sure that I'm encompassing a broad spectrum of anything and everything, that is in writing that listed terms and conditions between our company and the customer. There have been a few occasions where I operated under the assumption that the contract I had in my possession was the sole document governing the relationship, only to learn later that we had acknowledged a PO with vastly different terms.

INSURANCE COVERAGE

As we analyze each contractual provision in greater detail, we will see the critical role that insurance coverage plays at each step in the litigation process, but the impact of insurance that can be felt from the minute coverage is bound. Insurance issues can be very complex and can often confuse companies as to what they are covered for and what their true exposure may be. Many aspects of coverage such as deductible amounts, limits of coverage, and other preferences have to be decided upon after a thorough study of the business's needs and risks. But other issues can put the business in a very precarious position if coverage is inadequate or misunderstood. Without delving too deeply into the proper way to market your business to potential insurance carriers, and by the way that is how the process works, you want to establish early on that the carrier and broker has a thorough understanding of your company's operations and the services that you provide. Just as it is critical for outside defense counsel to know what makes the company tick, it is equally important, if not more so, for the insurance company to have a firm grasp on what the company's potential exposure is.

I have been purchasing insurance coverage on behalf of our company for almost 20 years. During that time I have killed and buried several dozen assumptions that I used to make when seeking new coverage, or renewing an existing policy. I no longer assume that certain things are covered, or that the insurance company knows what goals I'm trying to accomplish and what risks I'm trying to mitigate. It takes a straightforward and clear explanation as to what needs are present and what measures are available to meet those needs. An insurance policy is a unique product that does not always allow for an "apples to apples" comparison. I learned through several minor missteps, and a few major ones, that the amount of premium is but one factor to consider. What the policy covers, and what protections you will and will not have in the event of a claim, is your primary concern.

For example, many are alarmed to learn that in most situations general liability policies do not cover alleged claims for breach of contract, only tort actions. And while courts are increasingly looking at the injury complained of and surrounding work that forms the basis for the claim to determine insurance coverage, instead of dismissing out of hand anything framed as breach of contract, not knowing this fact could cause unknown exposure. Other areas of importance in insurance coverage include the treatment of additional insureds and granting certain waivers. It is a basic fact in the contracting experience that most of our customers will require additional insured status. This plays a very critical part in security litigation and must be dealt with directly from the outset. Knowing how insurance carriers approach the subject is very important to customer relations and to answer the question after the fact as to whether or not the customer truly held the status of being an additional insured. Many carriers employee a process of automatically granting additional insured under a blanket endorsement, but this typically requires that the contract at issue include this requirement. If it does not, then additional insured status may not be granted.

The handling of waivers of subrogation is also critical when evaluating insurance coverage. Many customers require subrogation to be waived. This essentially means that your insurance carrier is giving up the right to seek reimbursement from an allegedly responsible party, in this case your customer. Knowing exactly how these matters are handled by your insurance company is essential in drafting or agreeing to certain contractual terms. In each of these instances, additional insured and waivers of subrogation, the protection sought can only be accomplished, by not only having terms in the contract, but also having the proper endorsements on the insurance coverage.

Equally as important as coverage issues, and from a practical standpoint even more impactful, is knowing how insurance companies approach claims. I have been fortunate to work with the same insurance professionals for many years, so we have learned each other's processes, perspectives, and rhythms when it comes to processing and investigating claims. I'm very clear on how the process will take shape and what my obligations and responsibilities are in the area of claim reporting and investigation. I am also keenly aware of the impact this process can potentially have on the customer relationship, and do not hesitate to communicate these concerns when the situation calls for it. For example, I prefer to be informed prior to any letter or other form of communication being sent to the customer. It is not good for business to be blindsided with an angry phone call from the customer who wants to know why they are being asked to respond to an insurance claims representative they have never heard of. This often results in anxiety and unhealthy assumptions about the security services company's intentions to shift blame or seek some type of restitution from the customer. Insurance companies have a role to play and a job to do, but security services companies must make their expectations clear in regard to direct communication with the customer.

THE CONTRACT

Now that we have briefly examined some preliminary issues and routine challenges of the contracting process, let's look at an analysis of the contract itself. Once a decision is made to utilize a contract security company's services, the next logical step is the presentment of a document to memorialize the services that will be rendered. As we have already examined, this road can take many twists and turns, but regardless of whether or not you are in control of drafting the agreement, or if you are in a position to take the terms as they are or leave them, knowledge is the ultimate power. As we look at individual sections, do not lose sight of the fact that many times one provision can have a substantial impact on another, depending on how they are structured and the wording that is used. I liken contracts to a short story. The plot can often thicken the more you read, and the twists and turns of the story can have a huge impact on whether or not there is a happy ending.

The parties

The parties to the agreement may appear to be a foregone conclusion and not worthy of much discussion. However, this can be an area of consideration. In today's climate of acquisitions, conglomeration, and subsidiaries, it is not unheard of to see a previously unknown entity listed as the contracting party. I've experienced this on many occasions, primarily in the residential and retail property arena. We may be providing service to a specifically named residential complex or shopping center, but when the time to execute the contract arrives the party is either a real-estate firm or a property management organization. This can cause some confusion on the part of the security company who expected to be in direct contract with the property, but this in itself is not a cause for alarm. However, it could create later issues in the area of payment for services or insurance coverage.

When I receive a contract where the identified party is a previously unknown entity, or different from what was expected, I at minimum do some cursory research on the organization. I will also clarify what role the organization will play in funding the services and making decisions about the day-to-day operations. If my research uncovers a history of bankruptcies, numerous acquisitions of the same property, or other potential red flags, I will address this at the early stages of contract negotiations. On more than one occasion, I have found that we have supplied services at different locations to the same entity and have outstanding balances for nonpayment of services previously provided, or past insolvency. This again is a business decision, but knowing the true facts about the party you are entering into a relationship with will give you the information to make the decision.

Scope of work/duties and responsibilities

I have no substantial or scientific data to back this claim up, but based on my experience very few agreements devote more than a mere passing reference to the scope of work and duties expected of the security services provider. I am not an advocate for spelling out the post instructions or operating procedures in minute detail within the body of a contract since the orders should be a living, breathing, and evolving instrument, but it is advisable to at a minimum have a scope of work within the document. This can be done by giving a brief recitation in the body of the contract or attaching an exhibit outlining the basic duties. This serves two primary purposes: (1) to establish the framework of the services that are expected to be provided and (2) to establish who is responsible ultimately for creating the guidelines that are to be followed.

This in essence is an opportunity to give a contractual answer to whom "the decider" is, and just as important, what initial decisions have been made. These details can range from hours of service per week, locations of post, physical addresses if multiple properties are involved, whether or not the officer will be armed or unarmed, and the basic duties of the security officers. Equipment required to be furnished by the security company and other job-related requirements should also be included in this section. Consider the following sample clause that outlines each of these areas:

> *Security Company (Company) shall provide services, as more fully described in Exhibit "A" attached hereto and made a part hereof (collectively, the "Work"), in accordance with the terms and conditions set forth herein. The Work generally consists of on-site security guard services at Customer's facility located at 123 Elm Street New York, NY (the "Site"). All security officers will be licensed according to the current jurisdictional regulations and will be UNARMED. Service shall commence on January 1, 2016. WEEKLY HOURS OF SERVICE: Weekly hours of Service: 168. These hours will be deemed "normal". Normal hours can be changed upon one (1) day's written notice to company.*

In this scenario exhibit "A" can be drafted in conjunction with the customer to reflect the basic understanding of the post instructions and duties. In addition, a reference can be made to future comprehensive post instructions that will be developed by the customer and the security company upon mutually agreeing to the same. But as discussed previously, the divide between the status quo and current recommended enhancements should be addressed at this juncture. Unfortunately, the lines can quickly be drawn in negligent security suits and one of the key questions that will be asked is whether or not the security company, who will later be referred to as nothing short of an expert in all things related to making sure the property remains safe from outside elements, offered any solutions to mitigate known gaps in security coverage. While this often turns more on legal theory than it does on any actual malice, you can expect that the question will land squarely back in your lap. This can be addressed by inserting a few sentences in the initial agreement:

It is hereby acknowledged that customer is solely responsible for determining the set number of service hours per week, post locations, and is also solely responsible for issuing orders governing the security functions of the officers on duty.

In the alternative, Security Company is willing to conduct a security assessment analyzing the customer's property and offering recommendations in regards to number of weekly hours, post locations, and security duties.

Customer herby

_____ accepts Security Company's offer of a security assessment

Customer Initials: _____

_____rejects Security Company's offer of a security assessment

Customer Initials: _____

This language is admittedly a little pointed and direct, and when utilizing it you must assume that it will often be met with resistance. Consider the following case that I found myself at the center of after a parking lot shooting. Our customer was a large metropolitan city and the contract involved well over 100 unarmed security officers at various posts throughout the downtown area. One such location was a parking lot accessible to the public and business owners whose shops were located in a downtown business district. Despite the enormous size of the parking lot, the contract only allowed for one unarmed officer to be assigned to the location.

As with virtually all municipal, state, or federal contracts, the bid process consisted of very explicit requirements that were expected to be fulfilled by the successful contractor. The information provided to proposing companies was extensive and detailed down to the hours of service, location of posts, and even shift starting and end times. The initial package also included a thorough set of post instructions for each site with the mandate to carry those instructions out without deviation or modification. The only change that was allowable was replacing the logo of the previous security company with our own in the heading of the post orders. A clear case of the "status quo" being the only acceptable method for complying with contractual requirements.

One summer evening just after nightfall, a business owner was returning to the public parking lot to retrieve his car and go home for the night. While he was walking to his vehicle the security officer assigned to that location was performing her task as outlined by the city issued post operating procedures. While the business owner was walking to the south end of the parking lot the officer was stationed at the north end standing watch at the cashier's booth for the nightly cash transfer. When the soon-to-be victim reached his car he was approached by someone demanding the keys to his vehicle. The assailant emphasized this threat by brandishing a weapon. The victim then firmly refused his demands and initiated a physical struggle in an attempt to disarm the suspect. The end result was the victim being shot twice in the upper body, and while he suffered serious injury, he survived and eventually recovered with some lingering physical and mental impairments.

As with most incidents of this type, litigation was commenced rather quickly. We found ourselves as codefendants along with the city that had contracted for our services. As you might imagine, the key issue in the case was whether or not the parking lot was kept in a safe and secure manner, and what additional measures could have been implemented to prevent this tragic occurrence. As expected, the narrative quickly formed that this was preventable and but for the refusal of the city to allocate additional resources and provide additional security measures – including more officers, this would have never happened.

I sat through countless depositions, including my own, and heard this recurring theme stated in various forms. However, I was not entirely prepared for what I heard and witnessed when it came time for the city's representative to testify. I was certain that he would endure the same questions and tactics that I was subjected to, and I fully expected that he would respond by stating that they felt that reasonable security measures had been implemented taking all factors into consideration. But he decided to take a slightly different approach. To paraphrase, he left no doubt that it was the position of the city that our company was not only responsible for determining the levels of staffing and procedures that should be followed, but he also felt that we had failed in that regard.

While the case ultimately settled, as most do, I was put in the unenviable position of having to push back against a rather large and somewhat powerful customer. It was up to me at that point to prove that not only were we given no freedom to deviate from the stated staffing levels and preconceived security procedures, there was no interest in discussing or evaluating alternatives. Through the process of preparing for the case, this task was made considerably easier when an email was located, that had been sent to the customer by a former company manager, offering the services of an evaluation team to review citywide measures and offer recommendations for any identified vulnerabilities. This was met by a polite but direct rejection of the idea and a restatement of the requirements that were nonnegotiable and must be followed.

If you have any experience with government contracts at any level, you have already come to the conclusion that any proposed language about the acceptance or rejection of security assessments would likely not be up for consideration. But simple steps such as an email offer can be valuable when, or hopefully if, you are put in that position. There are also other methods that will achieve the same result outside the four corners of the contract.

I am currently engaged in a legal action that originated in response to a homicide in an upscale community. While still in the early stages, it is unmistakable that the lack of adequate security measures will once again be at the heart of the case. The account began over a decade ago and the salesperson has long since moved on to the other professional opportunities. In reviewing all the documents from the inception of the customer relationship to present day, I found some very interesting communications. There was no formal offer of a security assessment whereby the customer accepted or rejected the services, but there were several instances of unsolicited recommendations sent to the customer concerning certain perceived access control vulnerabilities. The intent of this advice was to suggest that the customer consider adding one additional post to an area of access that was unmanned. There is no documented response from the customer, but based on the fact that the position was never created, it is obvious that the suggestion was never acted upon.

Let me also emphasize what I believe to be a very critical point. Nothing is gained in the area of customer service by drawing battle lines or approaching the other side with an "us vs. them" mentality. In talking to several colleagues over the years about the issue of who is ultimately in control of deciding critical issues such as poststaffing and postprocedures, the most popular response is that it's a collaborative effort and both the security company and customer share the responsibility. That is by far the most enviable and productive relationship to strive for and achieve, but in the rough-and-tumble world of security litigation that relationship often takes a backseat to what becomes a new set of priorities.

I have spent my entire professional career working for a company that places the needs of the customer, and the survival of the customer relationship, above virtually anything else, even in some cases where it was detrimental to the best interests of the company. But I have also learned that as business professionals we must be prepared for what we will encounter when bad times come. Often when discussing a potential lawsuit or serious incident with a management employee in the field, I will present various scenarios that may occur if or when litigation arises. If I suggest that our company and the customer may at some point be at odds with certain issues or facts, I'm usually met with response that "he or she would never take that approach." They are identifying the customer as being a particular management contact that they have built a certain rapport with over the years. This is not a book about how to deliver excellent customer service, or maintain lifelong relationships in business, but I can say emphatically that nothing is more important in our industry than a meaningful connection to those who purchase our services. And just as I represent my employer, the professionals that we interact with at our customer locations are tasked with making sure that the best interests of their company are preserved and protected as well. But I always point out to our employees that when litigation arises, we will not be dealing with that singular individual at the customer location, rather we will be up against the interest of the corporation as whole, insurance companies, and other parties that may have conflicting goals. It is then when we are placed squarely in the position of defending ourselves and our services that we often realize that the only thing we can stand upon is the reliability of what we're in the business of selling.

TERM AND TERMINATION

When a lawsuit hits my desk, or when I get word that a significant event has occurred, my first priority is to get the governing contract in my hand. I need to know the "rules" we were playing by and what we can expect the respective parties to do in response. It is not uncommon for me to find an agreement that is several years old and has not been updated in the recent past. This can cause some initial alarm, but is not always a source of legitimate concern, if contracts have been drafted correctly. Most service contracts these days include automatic renewals, also known as evergreen clauses. These clauses seek to extend or renew the agreement for subsequent periods, if proper notice is not given by the parties. In these cases the service agreement can continue perpetually until cancelled.[3]

While there are times when the security company might want to avoid the use of auto renewal clauses, and these types of agreements are disfavored by consumer advocates when they are used in scenarios such as software licensing and cell phone contracts, they can serve to protect both parties and

---

[3]Certain states have enacted laws governing the use of automatic renewal clauses that seek to regulate their use, and force the language to be clear and conspicuous in the agreement.

to take away any debate as to whether or not a contract was in effect at the time. A typical auto renewal clause will resemble the following:

The initial term of this Agreement shall be for the term of three (3) years (the "Initial Term") commencing on the date this Agreement is executed. At the expiration of the Initial Term, this Agreement will automatically renew for successive one (1) year periods (each a "Renewal Term" and collectively with the Initial Term the "Term") unless a party provides the other parties with notice of its intent not to renew this Agreement at least ninety (90) days prior to the expiration of the then current term.

One variation on this language seen often in security service agreements does not include any "automatic renewal" wording, but rather states that the agreement will remain in effect until cancelled by various means that the contract describes. Typical cancellation clauses will anticipate events such as business insolvency, when the situation dictates that the customer no longer requires the service, or the property is sold. There are also provisions that allow for either party to cancel upon a written notice period, typically a minimum of 30 days, for any reason whatsoever. These are usually reasonable measures that can be taken if one or both parties do not see fit to contain the relationship. A conflict arises when cancellation provisions are drafted on a unilateral basis.

When one party has the exclusive right to cancel the contract, the other party, often the security services company, can suffer a variety of potential setbacks. First and foremost is the basic principal of contractual fairness. If one party can get out of the agreement, then why not the other? But often more practical considerations are at play as well. If you have signed a contract with a unilateral cancellation clause, also referred to as a rescission or termination for convenience clause, then you must ensure that you have the ability to cancel should the need arise, or face a potential breach of contract action. This can be an unwelcome addition to a tort claim that may be pending or anticipated.

I encountered an interesting set of facts when dealing with a unilateral cancellation clause recently. The contract gave the customer the sole right to cancel the agreement for any reason, and our company did not appear to have any avenue to pursue the same. This is a rare issue that I dive into since it is not typically a consideration when client retention is your goal. But I do find myself in this area when one particular issue arises: collections. Like all security companies, and any business owner for that matter, we occasionally encounter customers who can't, or for whatever reason won't, pay for the services that we render. As a last resort, we find it necessary to cease service due to this fact. One of the first steps in this process, along with researching potential collections actions, is to review the current contract. My attention is always drawn first and foremost to any cancellation provisions to see what the ground rules are. It is never a welcome sight to see a cancellation provision that is one-sided and does not allow for the company to give notice of cancellation. But of course, the nonpayment of agreed-upon rates is in itself a breach and should give the company the ability and right to cancel services. In most cases, this is not only logical but also legally correct. However, the situation got a little more interesting.

In addition to having a one-sided termination provision where the customer, and the customer only, was permitted to cancel with a short notice period, there were also certain provisions attached to the payment of invoices by the customer. The following clause was included in the contract:

> *Customer has the right to dispute any amounts owed to security company that in its sole discretion it deems to be for services that were not rendered as required by this agreement, or to withhold amounts due to security company to offset any damages resulting from the negligence of security company, or for reimbursement for damage to any customer owned equipment or property.*

The customer in the situation at hand was claiming certain amounts as authorized to be withheld in accordance with these provisions. So, the question posed by this set of facts was: If the customer is claiming an offset or otherwise disputable amount, are they in fact in breach of this agreement? A rather interesting situation certainly ensued, and although it was resolved ultimately in our favor, it would have at least resulted in a tangled legal scenario if an action was commenced.

From a business necessity standpoint, some security companies are reluctant to get updated contracts from year to year as this may push the project into an annual bidding scenario, so many accounts continue with agreements that are several years old. However, it is vital that the contract you are working under has language that allows it to survive from year to year, and gives the security company, as well as the customer, some ability to reasonably terminate should the need arise. A simple clause allowing each party this option will usually suffice:

> *CANCELLATION: Either party may cancel this Agreement at any time upon thirty (30) days written notice by Certified Mail. Notice for Company under this agreement shall be sent to _____. Notice for Customer may be sent to _____. The date the notice is postmarked shall serve as the beginning of the 30 day notice period.*

Choice of law/venue

I recently read an article in a sports periodical examining the benefits of home-field advantage in collegiate and professional sports. The author was making a strong case for the competitive advantage that teams enjoy by being in their native environment. These benefits range from the lack of travel stress to the atmosphere created by a large and loyal fan base that seeks to make it as miserable as possible for the visiting opponent. I would imagine that the location of competition is an issue that is routinely discussed, debated, and relentlessly pursued by coaches and sports executives. There is a reason that teams in some sports who perform well during the regular season are rewarded by securing some type of home-field advantage during the playoffs.

In addition to wanting to gain the upper hand in respect to where the games will be played, there is also great benefit derived from making sure the rules that govern the competition benefit your team. Each year prior to the college football season, and to a certain extent in the professional league, there seems to be an annual debate about some rule or regulation that needs to be adopted to conform to current playing styles. These issues sometime center around making the game more exciting for the fans, or addressing some perceived unfairness created by one team's ability to excel in a certain area to the detriment of their opponent.

These sports scenarios mirror what occurs in trial practice every day. Several years ago having been out of law school long enough to experience the real legal world, I was asked to speak to a group of aspiring lawyers and other legal professionals. One question that I was asked during my talk was "what is one thing you wish they would've taught you in law school that you've learned from experience?" I had my answer ready. I explained that while I had certainly learned the basics of jurisdictional issues in law school and the conflict that can arise when using different state laws, I had no concept of how vitally important these issues were and how impactful they can be to the success or failure of litigation. It was not until I started to encounter real lawsuits, in real courthouses, with real people that my eyes were opened to how the location of the stadium could impact the final score.

Sitting in a recent mediation session, with insurance representatives by my side, we began to go through the formalities of introductions and opening remarks. We were there to hopefully resolve a case that virtually everyone, with the obvious exception of the plaintiff, believed lacked any legal merit. However, as matters sometimes dictate, we were present to hopefully reach a good faith resolution that if successful would give neither party everything that they wanted. In preparation for this session, which was being spearheaded by our outside counsel, I had given little thought to the jurisdiction that the case has been filed in. But from the very minute the mediation commenced this fact was front and center and dominated the majority of the discussion. I must admit that it was more than a little unsettling to hear the mediator, who was very well respected and highly sought after due to his ability to bring parties together, tell us in no uncertain terms that due to the venue that a future trial would be held in, it was not a matter of if we would lose – only how badly the defeat would be. As I struggled to bring the conversation back to the facts of the incident and the applicable law, the focus always circled back to trial location. To be clear, in this scenario contractual provisions between our company and the customer would likely have had no impact due to the fact that the plaintiff was a third party, but this was a clear illustration that thought and planning should go into drafting these clauses or agreeing to what you are presented.

Most agreements that you will deal with will contain some type of provision, addressing what state law would be utilized when a dispute arises, and what the proper venue will be if an action should be commenced. Both of these areas could have a critical impact if you encounter a legal dispute with your customer. Let's first examine what these provisions mean and why they are included in contracts.

When parties agree to contractual terms one of the things they may potentially be agreeing to is where everyone will go to resolve disputes. When a certain jurisdiction is agreed upon by both parties that is where you will likely be traveling to pursue the matter. A typical jurisdiction provision will look similar to the following:

Both parties agree and consent that any legal disputes arising out of, or in connection with, this Agreement, or the services to be performed under the agreement, will be under the exclusive jurisdiction of the Courts of Dade County Florida.

At first glance these provisions do not appear to present an extremely difficult challenge, but even geography needs to be taken into consideration. In today's business travel environment, and our communication capabilities, this may be less of a concern, but a factor nonetheless. I have experienced several instances where I was planning to commence a collective action to recover monies owed, only to find a jurisdictional clause that may require me to travel hundreds of miles to litigate the dispute. This certainly had an impact on my decision regarding whether or not to move forward based on a cost/benefit analysis. While courts will often interpret these clauses and enforce them according to whether or not there is some connection to the state, if both parties clearly agree to submit themselves to the jurisdiction you must assume that that is where you will be headed.

But even more important can be the consideration given to the choice of law. When parties contract they often specify which state law would apply to govern disputes. I have often received puzzled looks from colleagues when I explain that the service may have been performed in Texas, but the lawsuit has been filed in Georgia, and Alabama law will be applied. That is a somewhat rare scenario, but certainly could occur based on the choice of law provision.

A common choice of law provision will spell out clearly what law is to be used:

> *This Agreement shall be governed by and construed under the laws of the State of Georgia, without giving effect to that state's conflict of laws provisions.*

As you can see, the simple clause also speaks to the issue of conflicting laws. Conflict of laws deals with choice of law when a legal action may involve the laws of more than one jurisdiction or state, and a court must determine which law is most appropriate to resolve the action. While it is ultimately up to the judge to decide the enforceability of any such provisions, professionally drafted and mutually agreed upon choice of law clauses or choice of jurisdiction agreements must be assumed to be valid, and you should be aware of any potential consequences they may bring. While I would be quite impressed with any legal expert that had a firm grasp and thorough knowledge of all relevant laws in each of our 50 states and how to apply them in every scenario, a competent attorney can be a powerful ally to research matters such as damages, discovery rules, and other procedural matters prior to you agreeing to submit yourself to laws and locations you are unfamiliar with.

ALTERNATIVE DISPUTE RESOLUTION

The battle cry of "let's sue" has echoed from boardrooms to law offices for hundreds of years. And while I cannot state with any authority that the time-honored tradition of seeking civil justice in our court systems is likely to erode in our industry anytime soon, the use of alternative dispute methods will likely bring a decrease in litigation involving customers and service providers.

It is not uncommon to find in security services contracts extra judicial measures included for the purposes of avoiding a quick trip to the courthouse when problems arise. Many business professionals will argue the merits of processes such as arbitration, or more informal methods to remedy conflicts, but the threshold issue is knowing what you are agreeing to and how it will be applied.

Most dispute resolution methods are outlined in a very clear and concise manner, and appear to be reasonable in their attempt to resolve conflicts prior to litigation becoming necessary, as this sample language indicates:

> *If there is any dispute regarding the rights or obligations of a Party arising hereunder, the Party asserting same shall provide written notice to the other Party (the "Notice of Dispute"). As soon as reasonably possible under the circumstances, the Parties shall agree to one of two (2) separate forms of informal dispute resolution: (1) the Parties may agree to conduct a telephone conference or meeting attended by representatives of each Party, or (2) in the alternative, the Parties may agree to conduct mediation at a time and place and pursuant to the rules mutually agreed to by the Parties. In the event the Parties do not resolve their dispute within ninety (90) days after the date of the Notice of Dispute or if reasonably necessary in order to prevent irreparable harm at any time prior thereto, either Party shall have the right to file an action regarding such dispute in any court of competent jurisdiction.*

The intent here is clear, the process is concise, and can be somewhat easily implemented if a dispute arises. Formal arbitration clauses with detailed steps and responsibilities of both parties in the event of submitting disputes are also gaining popularity in security services agreements. These, and other similar alternatives, could potentially save the time and expense of litigation and resolve the dispute to both parties' satisfaction. But the inclusion of this language can be an unwelcome surprise if one party, primarily the security company, is not aware of its existence prior to filing litigation. The key once again is to know what you agreed to prior to having a need to use it.

Indemnification/hold harmless

If the security services agreement was a Hollywood movie, the indemnification language would play the starring role. Depending on which side of the table you find yourself on, it could appear as either the hero that swoops in and saves the day, or the despised villain whose mission is to wreak havoc and relentlessly seek to destroy those who come in its path. A carefully worded indemnification agreement can strike fear in the heart of the one whose duty it may be to indemnify, or it can bring a sense of reassuring comfort to a party that has just realized that they may have a way out after all. Throughout my career I have witnessed a multitude of situations where indemnification and hold harmless agreements were not just an issue in security litigation, but they were *the issue*. Unfortunately, they are often misunderstood and misapplied, even by the parties that initially agreed to the terms. The potential legal and financial consequences for a security company cannot be understated in the area of indemnification and hold harmless clauses. I have witnessed far too many assumptions shattered at the hands of the judge or jury when the prevailing party is allowed to take financial cover in the midst of a legal battle, at the expense of the other.

I want to be clear that indemnification plays an important part in contract law in general, and security services relationships specifically, and should not be viewed as entirely negative or burdensome. If I were a General Counsel working for a large, or for that matter a small, corporation seeking to acquire security services, one of my top contractual priorities would be making sure that we have sufficient protections in place if negligent services are rendered that results in some type of loss. In that same vein, one of my top priorities in my present role is making sure our company is shielded from accepting unreasonable responsibility and obligations that go far beyond those that are within our ultimate control. This is an admittedly difficult and lofty goal at times, and just as we have already discussed, can be complicated if bargaining power is not equitable, but once again information is key when dealing in this critical area. The language of the indemnity clause is very important. When does the obligation arise? Does it cover legal fees or just damages? What happens if more than one party is at fault? As I have seen happen on several occasions, the time to answer these questions is not after you get sued, but before you sign the contract.

Let's start by taking a look at what indemnification is truly designed to accomplish. A standard indemnification clause seeks to obligate one party to compensate and shield the other party from any losses or damages. The duty to indemnify can be undertaken by both parties, or the clause can be drafted to significantly favor one party over another. An indemnitor is the party who is obligated to pay another. An indemnitee is the party who is entitled to receive the payment from the indemnitor. Indemnification provisions are a way for our customers to shift risk to the security services company, and while less frequent, from security services company to the customer.

The obligations undertaken in this regard can include cost to defend an action, eventual court verdicts, and virtually any financial loss suffered by the indemnified party. In the same way, hold harmless agreements can severely limit the security company's ability to allocate any of the risk to the customer. Many courts and legal experts combine indemnification and hold harmless agreements as one contractual issue. They are very similar in content and often have the same result, but they will on occasion be presented as two separate provisions or in some cases, there can be an entirely separate hold harmless agreement. While they are often combined, hold harmless provisions act as a method that releases the indemnitee from liability to the indemnitor. Essentially one party is saying that they don't want to have the burden of being concerned about a lawsuit from the other party to the contract. I have seen these presented buried in "contractor safety packets" or in "annual updates to your vendor profile." You can imagine the frustration of an attorney who has spent a substantial amount of time to negotiate a contract they can live with, only to have an employee unknowingly sabotage the process by signing a conflicting agreement a few months later. Depending on the language used to outline the hold harmless duties and depending on the context of the event that gives rise to indemnification, the payment of the attorney's fees can take up a sizable portion of the financial commitment owed to the other party.[4] And while all contractual provisions should be carefully crafted and diligently scrutinized, this is never more critical than in the area of indemnification and hold harmless responsibilities. Accepting indemnification responsibility essentially means that you are becoming the insurance provider for your customer. Since you are being asked to cover losses it is imperative that you know what triggers that obligation. By agreeing to an overly broad indemnification clause, your company can be assuming a wide array of liability, some of which may go well beyond your insurance coverage.

This is an area where real-world application is critical to understand the potential consequences, but let's first examine how the simple inclusion or removal of a certain wording can change the complexity and meaning of an indemnification clause. This area of contract law has dominated a large majority of the time that I have spent over the years negotiating contracts with customers. On multiple occasions when attempting to reach a compromise on language I have been told by customer representatives or outside counsel that they simply want to ensure that they have ample protection from suits and damages that result from our negligence. An admirable goal and one that most would not quarrel with. But behind that broad legal philosophy lurks many legal twists and turns that begin and often end with the contract itself. The indemnification provision of an agreement is interpreted under the same rules governing any other contracts, with a view to determining the intent of the parties. The rights and duties of the indemnitor and indemnitee

---

[4]Some states, such as Illinois, do not allow for attorney's fees or other costs of defense as part of the indemnity agreement, unless it is expressly stated in the agreement and there is no duty to defend. Under the laws of most states, an indemnitor generally has no duty to defend unless the contract specifically requires such defense. The opposite is true in California where the duty is assumed unless the language in the contract expressly states otherwise.

are generally determined from the express terms of the contract itself.[5] So courts will rarely concern themselves with the fact that you may not like the result, they will typically only look to what you agreed to.

The following example illustrates how a simple modification, or addition, can radically change the obligations:

Sample Provision #1

Company shall indemnify and hold harmless the Customer, its agents and employees (hereinafter referred to collectively in the singular as "Indemnitee") from and against any loss, damage, injury liability, claim or lien for injury to person or property, or death of a person, resulting from the negligence or willful misconduct of company in the performance of company's work herein.

Sample Provision #2

Company shall indemnify and hold harmless the Customer, its agents and employees (hereinafter referred to collectively in the singular as "Indemnitee") from and against any loss, damage, injury liability, claim or lien for injury to person or property, or death of a person, resulting from the sole negligence or willful misconduct of company in the performance of company's work herein.

By carefully reviewing both the clauses, one minor variation is present. In sample provision number one, the security company is obligating itself to indemnify the customer from various losses resulting from the negligence or willful misconduct that could be attributable to it. In sample provision number two, the introduction of the word "sole" prior to "negligence" can largely negate this obligation in many situations. If the damage in question is not caused by the security company's sole negligence, there may be no indemnification obligation if this is in the agreement. Even if the damages were caused by an occurrence where the security company is mostly negligent, but it can be argued or claimed that the customer was also negligent in some fashion, there may be no duty to indemnify.

In contrast to this example, where a security company has his crafted language that would make it difficult for the customers to take advantage of indemnity in many situations, there are also trouble spots to be aware of that can expand its potential liability to an unreasonable level. When reviewing

---

[5]Crawford v. Weather Shield Mfg., Inc., 44 Cal. 4th 541, 552 (2008); Gibbs-Alfano v. Burton, 281 F.3d 12, 15-16 (2d Cir. 2002); Weissman v. Sinorm Deli, 88 NY 2d 437, 446 (NY, 1996).

indemnification clauses, one of the threshold issues when events occur is whether or not the obligation was triggered by some occurrence. Let's consider the following clause and the ramifications it could have for a security company:

> *Company agrees to indemnify, defend, and hold harmless Customer, its agents, employees and officers, from any and all liability, cost, or expense, including but not limited to attorneys' fees, arising out of or relating in any way to the performance of its Work, regardless of whether caused in part by the acts or omissions of Company. Nothing herein shall be interpreted as obligating Company to indemnify Customer against its sole negligence or willful misconduct.*

An interesting set of circumstances can rise from clauses drafted in this manner. The goal of this indemnification obligation is to have the duty to defend and hold harmless triggered by an endless set of potential circumstances. By attaching the responsibility of the security company to any situation that could be remotely tied to its services, the customer is greatly increasing the number of potential situations where the duty to indemnify would be invoked. Consider the broadness of events that could be characterized as "arising out of or relating in any way to the performance of its work." This could encompass virtually any incident, suit, or claim that resulted in injury or loss on the property.

One example from my past experience illustrates how broad indemnification clauses can be applied to the security company's detriment. While performing patrol services at a large transportation site, one of our officers suffered a medical event that resulted in a loss of consciousness. Subsequently, he was involved in a one-vehicle accident in the course of his duties. After the accident, all appropriate steps were taken to initiate a Workmen's Compensation (WC) claim and an investigation was commenced. During the course of the claims process an attorney was retained to represent the employee's interest in the WC matter. As is typical, minor legal controversies ensued and outside counsel was retained through our insurance carrier to represent our company in the matter. Seeking several documents and a copy of video footage of the accident, I was contacted by our WC counsel to assist in retrieving this information. When I contacted our customer, who was in possession of some of the information sought, I was given the standard reply that all such requests would have to pass through the legal department via a subpoena for proper vetting prior to the release of the documents and video footage. A reasonable process to employ when dealing with matters concerning a vehicle accident that occurred on your property.

As I later learned, the matter was sent to an outside counsel working on behalf of our customer. After having several discussions with him concerning preservation of evidence, privileges they felt needed to be asserted to protect certain information, and other basic and fundamental issues that surround these types of incidents, he also informed me that we would be expected to cover any and all expenses related to responding to our counsel's request for information in the underlying WC claim. It took a few seconds for this statement to register, but I quickly realized he was intent on applying our indemnification obligation to the matter at hand. Our contractual agreement in effect at the time had very similar language to the "arising out of or relating in any way to the performance of its work" example cited previously in this chapter. After a review of the current agreement, I began to construct a scenario in my mind that could potentially lead to a dizzying legal circle of liability that would always begin and end on our doorstep.

Since our current services agreement included this broad form of indemnification, we could theoretically be obligated to pay for any loss or expense incurred by the customer in any way related to the performance of our services – including a vehicle accident involving one of our employees. I then tried to make sense of the irony of this situation that ostensibly did not involve the customer as a party, except as a source of information. I could almost hear our WC attorney assigned to this case question my sanity as I laid out the scenario I was faced with. Each time he made a formal or informal request for documents from the customer, I would receive a bill for the time they spent on complying with the same. At the time of our conversation our obligation was approaching five figures with no end in sight. I was then forced to put him in the unenviable position of being very selective with his phone calls and letters to my customer as I was now paying the tab.

There are other far more serious and potentially damaging examples I could cite regarding broad indemnification provisions, but this occasion illustrates how virtually any situation can theoretically be made to fit into this broad definition. That is why it is essential to restrict any agreement to indemnify to the security companies negligence or willful misconduct. That ensures that fairness will flow not only to you, but also to your customer as well. By agreeing to indemnify the other party only for your missteps and mistakes, that is, your own negligence, you can avoid catastrophic claims in the future. One such case will live in my memory for many years.

It is the phone call that we all fear one day we might receive. An officer has been lost. Thankfully I was fortunate to work in this business for many years without dealing with the tragedy of one of our own losing their life in the course of duty. When you first hear these words concerns over future lawsuits, WC claims, and tasks such as OSHA reporting take a backseat – as they should. My initial concern was for his family and those he was leaving behind. The following days and weeks were devoted to finding out exactly what had occurred and managing other necessary tasks such as the WC process. Once the initial shock and grief began to subside, there of course was some thought to what legal realities the future would hold. We gladly satisfied our WC obligation to his dependent, and at that point felt that we had met our responsibility as a company. During the investigation of this accident, I did take the occasion to review the current services agreement, specifically the indemnification provisions. The language was pretty clear, we were to indemnify our customer only in cases of our own negligence. Nothing I had seen at that point, or as I recall the events now, led me to believe that this duty should be invoked.

After some time had passed, a wrongful death action was filed by the estate of the deceased employee against our customer. We were neither named in the action, nor were any negligence acts or misconduct claimed to have been committed our company. The allegations centered upon the actions taken by the customer that had preceded the tragic accident that took our employee's life. Nevertheless, the customer sought indemnification from our company for full defense costs and any eventual judgment. This resulted in a protracted legal conflict that lasted for several years. There were other issues at play as well, but the core argument landed on the indemnification provision. The only reason we had a viable defense in this case, that carried with it a rather large financial stake for our company if we did not in fact prevail, was due to the limited scope of the indemnification provision. Outcomes in court often times have less to do with what happens at trial, and everything to do with what happened when the contract was agreed to.

This case also involved another question concerning the obligations of a security company who undertakes an obligation to indemnify: Who is covered? It is not unusual to see a multitude of parties included under the right of indemnity. There may be parties that you have never heard of and you could be surprised to find out later that you may even be granting this right to actions against individual employees of the customer. A sample clause may include:

> *ABC Company, its directors, its officers, its employees, its agents,*
> *its stockholders and all related Affiliates.*

In this scenario, you may be forced to provide legal cover to potentially hundreds of parties should the need arise. In the previous wrongful death example, individual defendants, some who had since left the employ of our customer, were seeking to have full rights of indemnity applied to his legal situation. By agreeing to a broad category of covered parties, there are multiple scenarios where this could be a reality.

The obligation of an indemnitor is not to be taken lightly. The agreements that you make should always correspond with your current insurance coverage so you do not take on any independent financial obligation outside of what your policy will allow. Your role when the duty is brought to fruition is to hopefully only serve as a means to provide your insurance coverage to appropriate claims, not put your company on the hook for unrealistic exposure. Some labor under the incorrect assumption that simply because you agree to do something in a contract, insurance coverage will naturally always follow. This is not the case. The obligation you undertake to indemnify your customer can be seen as separate and distinct from any insurance policy you may carry. As we will see when we examine how to survive when lawsuits occur, there may be times when insurance companies make decisions not to assume the indemnification obligation. In those cases you may find yourself in the direct line of fire when the customer asks for your commitment to cover losses irrespective of the insurance coverage available. This presents a situation where far more is on the line than contract issues; your future relationship is at stake.

As always, a component attorney is an invaluable resource to guide you through the maze of current state laws and court interpretation, but since the issue of indemnity and hold harmless agreements are so vital to the contracting process, the following basic checklist will be a helpful tool when evaluating contracts beyond your own standard agreement:

Does the contract include not only an indemnity obligation but also hold harmless and an express duty to defend clause?

Are the indemnitee's legal fees and costs of defense included within the scope of indemnity?

Are the types of claims identified? (Third Party Claims, bodily injury or death, etc.)

Who are you required to cover? (Customer's affiliates, officers, directors, employees, agents, contractors, etc.).

Is my duty to indemnify limited to the security company's own negligence, or does it encompass acts committed by the customer?

Beware of "in connection with" or "arising out of" language as this may be broadly construed and connect the obligation with a variety of potential claims.

Is the indemnity clause consistent with my current insurance coverage, and other contractual clauses?

WHO CAN SIGN

I will close this discussion on contract terms with one reoccurring theme I have dealt with over the years, and an issue I have been asked about many times: Who has the power to sign an agreement? Companies are legal entities, but of course the company itself cannot sign agreements, so they rely on its agents to carry out certain acts. We have all likely experienced a situation where an overly eager sales person "closes a great deal" by proudly signing his name to a lengthy contract, without taking the time to have it reviewed, or for that matter read it themselves. Or a helpful mid-level manager who is happy to accommodate a loyal customer who just needs to "update the records" by getting a new agreement on file for the next fiscal year. When I have been faced with this dilemma, often after something significant has come to light and the contract search begins, I have been offered several reassuring words intended to ease my legal headache. "Don't worry Eddie, no one ever gave him permission to sign that contract, so we are fine" or "It is clear in our policy that you are the only one that can execute agreements, so the customer had no authority to ask him to do it". I appreciate these sentiments, but they hold no real legal value.

You may encounter some legal agreements that require a specific person to sign, or allow a certain group, such as bona fide company officers, to sign. This is seen routinely in large municipal contracts, when purchasing vehicles, or signing insurance agreements. But in most cases it can be anyone purporting to represent your company. This is a critical legal and internal training issue, because in most cases the signature of an employee will be deemed effective.

The general law of agency dictates that unless the party on the other side (your customer) is on notice that the party does not have contracting authority, the signature will bind the company to the terms of the contract. But you have not given them that authority? Unfortunately that question is irrelevant since most of your employees will fall into certain categories of authority. The first is obvious: they had the authority vested in them by their company. This may be by virtue of by-laws established by the company, a list of authorized signatories, or even possessing a valid power of attorney on behalf of the party. This requires little discussion since there is no debate as to whether the authority existed. The next level of authority is that which is implied by virtue of position or responsibility. If someone is, or holds themselves out to be, in a managerial capacity it can reasonably be assumed that they had the authority to bind the company and their signature will most likely be held as binding. I encounter this situation when dealing with people engaged in the "telephonic sales" industry.

Each year I send out a standard warning about conducting business over the phone or responding to unsolicited offers for goods and service. When these invoices, which by the way are often outrageously priced for the goods or services they claimed to have provided, land on my desk to deal with I am very familiar with the following routine. I will call the entity seeking to collect the money in exchange for listing our company on some obscure website, or for our recurring monthly order of office supplies in perpetuity, and explain that the order was neither desired nor authorized. On cue, they will then allow me to listen to a purported recording of the actual phone call that formed the basis of the "order". Without fail, the first line of the sales-person's script is to ask the person that answers the phone their name and title, and then repeat, "so you are Fred Jones Regional Manager" followed by an affirmation from the unsuspecting party on the other end. This is done to establish at minimum the party on the other end had implied authority to bind the company to these ridiculous orders. Due to the fact that I wish to keep the content of this book appropriate for readers of all ages, I will not describe the follow-up dialogue that typically occurs at this point when I am told that our company has entered into a valid contract and therefore owes some ridiculous sum, but you get the point. Whether you know it or not, or like it or not, your employees have the power to bind the company to agree-ments big and small.

It is critical to have a clear policy on who is allowed to sign agreements and who is not. As you have seen, a key step in the process is a thorough review by a competent party. The first step in this process is getting the agreement in the proper hands before signature. Make this part of new management training and lay out very clear expectations that are reviewed from time to time. I have found myself in several situations where I have had to make un-comfortable phone calls to outside counsel informing them of the discovery of a previously unknown agreement that was signed without my knowledge; make sure you avoid the same fate.

Rules are important. They are the guiding force throughout the life of a case. As you navigate the waters of security litigation, they will come to the surface time and time again, so make sure you know what is lurking in the shadows and never allow yourself to be overly surprised by terms and conditions that were previously not a concern. Information is key, and as we approach the time when the lawsuit arrives, what you know, and what you don't, can hurt you.

Chapter 4

You've been served: are we in this together?

I have been asked on many occasions: "can we get sued for this?" This inquiry usually comes on the heels of an incident that invokes fear and anxiety in business owners and company mangers alike. Unfortunately, concerns over liability and litigation many times will take precedence over improving the overall security environment and what lessons can be learned after a major incident. Our modern society has taught us that the threat of litigation is something to be feared above all else and we must constantly keep our guard up against those who seek to financially destroy our companies through the court system. I'm always saddened to hear stories concerning competitors and colleagues who lie awake at night wondering if this will be "the one" that drives them out of business. We have all been in this position where our only option is to play out possible scenarios that involve juries who are seemingly unsympathetic to companies, and vengeful plaintiffs who are ready to expose the slightest innocent misstep to highlight the need for financial justice. And I am sure there is a book or an article being written somewhere to address, once again, the need for meaningful tort reform and a system that allows the "winner" not to suffer financial ruin as a result of defending a frivolous action. This is not that book. The reality is that you can't ultimately control when or where you will be sued. Sure, there are steps that can be taken, ones hopefully you will find in these pages, to diminish the likelihood of lawsuits being filed against you or your customer, but at the end of the day, if someone wants to sue you - they will. I have irritated and frustrated many supervisors and colleagues alike, when on the heels of a major event the conversation ultimately flows to the question of what is next. Then the big worry comes in the form of a question that ends with: "we can't get sued for this, right?" After being in this business as long as I have, my standard response is "of course we can, and likely will, but let's talk about making it tough for someone to be successful if they decide to try."

There are several reasons that would cause an aggrieved party to decide to file a lawsuit against a security company. I believe the main reason is simple. We are security. We are perceived to be the entity that is present to make sure bad things don't happen. To a victim of crime, the logical person to blame is the security officer, and by extension, the company. "If they would have been performing their job properly, I would not have been victimized" is the most common theme and one that will be repeated many times during the life of a case. And while I would disagree with this philosophy in most of the cases I have been involved in, it is however a logical reason. Many perceive measures employed for the purpose of deterring and detecting activity as a guarantee that such activity will not occur. Those engaged in the security industry, and most people with a reasonable amount of life experience, know that this is an unrealistic assumption to make. But that is what we are often faced with when trying to craft a viable defense.

To make matters worse, defendants often feel forced to settle lawsuits, even if they feel like the law is on their side, simply because the cost of legal fees and risk of big awards is too high to warrant fighting back. It can be argued that this ultimately encourages even more lawsuits. I have even seen recently that security-related lawsuits have become an area of specialty with targeted adverting directed toward those individuals who have "been a victim of crime that could have been prevented by adequate security measures." The advertisement usually goes on to describe the various means by which the victim can recover. Add to this the complication that there are no true federal standards for security services and lawsuits are governed by various state laws, it can be an overwhelming problem.

Even though the reality of lawsuits can seem daunting, it is also a basic fact that not every crime victim can successfully sue by merely proving that he or she was injured at a location where a security company had some individuals present. Instead, civil liability only arises when the plaintiff can establish that a security company failed to exercise reasonable care in providing needed security and that this failure caused or contributed to the injuries suffered by the crime victim.

The four basic elements of a security-related lawsuit are:[1]

1. The victim, or injured party, had a right to be on the premises either as an employee, visitor, tenant, or customer.
2. The customer or security service provider either owed a legal or contractual duty to exercise reasonable care to make the premises safe.

---

[1]States laws vary on what is required to be proven to establish negligence in a security-related suit. Issues such as apportioning fault to the perpetrator of a crime, contributory negligence, and damages are issued that may be treated differently depending on state statutes and case law.

This naturally flows into what the responsibilities were of the customer and the security services provider to implement measures to make the environment safe and secure.

3. The customer and/or the security services provider negligently failed to implement security measures necessary to make the premises reasonably safe and protect the victim from injuries that were sustained at the hands of a criminal, an employee, or even a visitor. This is where many security lawsuits can be won or lost. What measures did the customer and/or security company take versus the measures they should have implemented? This is also where foreseeability is critical as the security company and customer will be judged based on the reaction they had and the measures implemented in response to prior incidents.

4. Finally, the injured party must show that the negligence of the customer and/or Security Company was the proximate cause of the injury. In other words, if additional measures would have been taken, if additional officers would have been present, if access control would have been tighter, the injury likely would not have taken place. This of course is extremely subjective and the facts of each case can present unique challenges.

Using these basic elements, security companies can develop a roadmap to proactively defending future litigation. Each element can highlight the need to thoroughly examine what security measures need to be taken, and what measures are in fact implemented in light of what may come in the future. From past experience, I can attest to the fact that virtually every step that is taken in the course of deciding a comprehensive security plan will be scrutinized with emphasis on past events and the likelihood of future success. This may seem to be an unreasonable and impossible standard to achieve, but the key is to diligently document your efforts and the data they are ultimately based on.

FIRST THINGS FIRST

But before we dive headfirst into the reality of lawsuits, let's take a step back and examine what reaction is necessary when an incident occurs. I can remember a day several years ago standing with a colleague looking out at hundreds of boxes containing daily activity reports, incident reports, and other assorted documents that were generated by security officers and management employees. Just in this one area of our secure records storage alone, the boxes easily contained hundreds of thousands of pages. Seeking to make the most effective use of our space, the following question was posed to me: "do you really need all of these documents?" My response was simple "No. Statistically speaking, I will probably only ever need a

100 pages out of this vast mountain of information. But the problem is - I have no idea which ones." Just as with those documents, you never truly know which incidents will or will not lead to litigation. I have dozens of examples of seemingly innocent occurrences that lead to major events, but one such incident I have always found to be a great illustration on how things can change in an instant.

If you were to ask the average citizen, or even a group of security professionals, if they are familiar with a man named Frank Wills and the impact he had on the course of American history, most would not immediately recognize the name. But the story of a 24-year-old security officer is one of the best illustrations of how seemingly insignificant situations can evolve into life-changing events. In June of 1972, Wills was working as a security officer at an office building and residential complex. The location was not a very well known landmark at the time and Officer Wills' duties consisted of patrolling the building and keeping watch for anything unusual. In the 1 year that Officer Wills had worked here, there had been only one attempted burglary, so he was not used to dealing with too much drama.

During his rounds on the night of June 17, 1972 Officer Wills noticed a piece of duct tape on one of the door locks of an office suite. The tape appeared to have been placed over the latch bolt to prevent the door from locking when shut. Not thinking much of it, he removed the tape and continued on his patrol. Thirty minutes later, Wills came back to the door and he noticed there was more tape on the door. At this point, Willis notified the authorities who later responded to the scene to investigate these suspicious circumstances. That seemingly boring post where Officer Willis worked? The Watergate Hotel and Office Building. Unknown to Officer Willis at the time, but his "routine" observations and reactions had just started a chain of events that would ultimately lead to the downfall of the most powerful man in the world with the resignation of President Nixon just 2 years later. I am certain that Officer Willis could never have imagined when he clocked into work on that fateful day that his patrol log would be a central document in the greatest political scandal in US History, and that one day his handwritten entries would occupy a place of prominence in the National Archives.[2]

I have used the story of Frank Willis many times in report writing classes and training presentations to illustrate how proper documentation can play a vital role in defending lawsuits. But this also proves the point that you truly never know what incidents will develop into a lawsuit, and which ones will

---

[2]Security Officer's Log of the Watergate Office Building Showing Entry for June 17, 1972: https://research.archives.gov/id/304970

just fade away. Success or failure in future actions begin in the minutes, hours, and days following the occurrence that may give rise to a future action. At this point in my career I still struggle with which events are serious, and which ones should not be a cause for alarm. The simple reality is I have seen many that I was almost guaranteed would result in litigation that never did, and conversely I have reviewed incidents that did not elicit even a second look, only to find myself in court a year later taking that second look. I firmly believe that hoping for the best and planning for the worst is an excellent guiding principle when dealing with internal incidents and events that have any measure of liability that could result in a claim or lawsuit.

It is imperative that you establish an internal process for the purpose of identifying incidents and investigating the same. I would also encourage you not to deviate from the process or be swayed by internal or external voices that will tell you "don't worry about this one, nothing will ever come of it." I have fallen prey to that temptation on more than one occasion, only to be scrambling many months later in an attempt to gather a reasonable amount of information after the lawsuit arrives. This is dangerous from a number of different standpoints. First, memories fade. I can assure you, based on past experience, that it is not ideal to have a security officer attempt to write a report concerning an event that may have occurred several months, or even years, in the past. This is especially true if the occurrence in question would not have automatically been seen as a "major" incident at the time. I have been involved in numerous cases where the security officers observations or actions at the time were viewed as routine and insignificant, only to play a key role in the defense of future litigation.

Another key factor to consider in the establishment of an internal process of documenting and investigating incidents is that the parties involved may not remain in your employ by the time the situation evolves into a lawsuit. A significant amount of time and resources are routinely devoted to tracking down former security officers and management employees when lawsuits arise in the future. While there is no way to predict exact turnover, by responding effectively to the incident at the time of occurrence, a solid foundation of information can be cataloged and documented for future use. I have been in the unenviable position of not knowing exactly what a former security officer or management employee actually knew about the situation; much less what I was anticipating them to say in a deposition or on the stand. Surprises are rarely good in lawsuits, and without a solid process in place; surprises are typically what you will get.

Just as making sure reports are secured, and employee statements are preserved for the future, overall document and evidence retention is key in future lawsuit defense. As we will see later in the context of discovery, after you've been served is not the ideal time to attempt to gather all relevant documents. You will find many have been disposed of, or are now in sole possession of the customer, or for whatever reason are no longer available to the security company. It has never filled me with confidence to reach out to an internal employee to request things such as post orders, several months of daily activity reports, and other relevant documents after a lawsuit has been filed, only to find that "were not real sure anyone bothered to keep those items." That is the very definition of starting out on the wrong foot.

Interwoven throughout the process of documenting officer observations and securing any evidence, is the notification and involvement of the insurance company. While policy language, and other known rules and procedures will govern the technicalities of reporting, it is imperative that a rapport is established between the security company and the insurance claims representatives. I have been fortunate to work with some of the same insurance professionals over a long period of time and have become accustomed to the process of reporting and investigating. I have also reached a level of comfort that allows me to express concerns about how the process may be handled and what impact may be potentially felt by our customer. One key consideration is the threat of losing coverage, or the ability to effectively defend an action, by not reporting the matter early on. Without delving too deeply into the economic science of loss runs, claim reserves, and other factors that can impact the overall cost your insurance program, some companies are reluctant to report every occurrence to their insurance carrier. While this is solely an internal decision, you must weigh certain risks before deciding not to file a claim. The most obvious risk is loss of coverage when the claim is not timely reported, but there is also a more practical issue involved.

Notifying the insurance company at the earliest stage will not only allow you the comfort of having an official claim open, it will also establish an investigative record from day one. I have spoken to several companies in the past who are adverse to the concept of filing every potential claim for reasons associated with the investigative process. There are fears that the customer will be directly contacted, or insurance investigators will begin to invade the work environment. Some also express a desire to avoid endless requests from the insurance company for information related to the event such as contracts, post orders, and personnel files. I can understand these concerns; I sympathize with the goal of not creating any unnecessary friction with the customer, or extra work for the security company. However, I believe that if an incident occurs it is best to take these steps as the reward certainly outweighs the perceived risk.

One of the most overlooked aspects of negotiating insurance coverage is getting a feel for the policies and procedures that the carrier follows. That's why I wholeheartedly believe that it is important to select a carrier that is not only familiar with the security services industry, but specializes in it. There is no substitute for many years of experience in dealing with unique security services matters, and also the business intelligence necessary to know how it can impact our customer base. But this knowledge is not automatic and cannot be assumed. While some security companies merely look at premiums, coverage proposed, and whether or not the limits are adequate, there should also be a process to evaluate the claims management and investigative process. How are claims reported? What is the turnaround time from the initial report to the first contact from a claims representative? What basic information will routinely be requested from the security company over the life of the investigation? How long does a typical investigation take? These questions, and others, should be asked prior to selecting a policy. The time to know these answers are before the relationship begins, not after you are standing side-by-side trying to fend off a lawsuit.

Over the years, I have established an internal checklist with steps that need to be taken in response to an occurrence or event that may give rise to litigation.[3] Many of these steps may be actually performed by insurance representatives, investigators hired by the insurance company, our outside counsel. However, each step is vital and should be addressed:[4]

> *Contracts*: Secure a copy of the contract in effect at the time of the occurrence. This may be in the form of written agreement signed by both parties, or a purchase order or similar document. If applicable, always check with the local branch office to ensure that you have the most relevant and recent agreement.
>
> *Post Orders*: Secure a copy of the post orders in effect at the time of the occurrence. This should include any modifications communicated through emails from the customer, memos posted at the worksite, or recorded in pass-down logs.
>
> *Daily Activity Reports*: Secure copies of all daily activity reports for the location in question, and the date of the occurrence. (It is also a good practice at this point to make sure that the reports prior to an after the occurrence are being maintained as well.)

---

[3]This checklist is also included as Appendix E.
[4]In order to sufficiently protect documents and statements from being legally discoverable in the future, always consult with an in-house counsel or outside attorney on the proper procedure for creating statements, reports, or other evidence in anticipation of litigation.

Incident Reports: Secure copies of all incident reports. If the officer did not complete an incident report, or the report is not adequate, have those involved make written statements describing their activities prior to, during, and after the occurrence. It is also a good practice to question those who are involved to elicit information that may not be found within the written reports.

Patrol Recording Data: Inquire about the presence of any tour-recording device that may show where the officer was prior to, during, and after the occurrence.

Witness Statements: Secure witness statements from anyone that may have observed the actual occurrence, or related activities. If the witnesses are employees of your customer, seek permission from the customer representative prior to contacting any witnesses.

Video Footage: Inquire about the presence of video recording in the area of the occurrence or in the surrounding environment. Secure a copy of the recording when possible. Just as with witness statements, in most cases customer permission will be needed prior to accessing any video storage system.

Payroll Records: Print out or store payroll records showing the times and dates officers worked. This should include the date of the occurrence with all shifts (before and after). It is also a good practice to not only print out prepared schedules, but also secure actual time records showing who reported for duty.

Media Coverage: If applicable, keep copies of press coverage related to the occurrence. This is also an excellent time to remind all involved of the internal policy on media relations. Remember that any statements made can come back to haunt you later in the process. I have also seen comments made by the customer or other parties to the media that could assist in our defense. Always direct communication to a designated corporate representative with media training. Nothing is worse for public relations, and a potential legal defense, than the picture of an officer running away from TV cameras or making the wrong statement that implies that there is a scandalous secret lurking behind the scenes. It is always tempting to respond to inaccuracies in an effort to repair any damaging information spread by the media, but simple phrases such as "We are currently investigating the incident to determine what occurred and will be taking appropriate steps when the investigation is concluded" or "We are in the process of reviewing the lawsuit and will be responding through the proper legal channels" are advisable in many situations.

Police Reports: Get copies of police reports, if applicable. These reports often contain valuable information that would not otherwise be obtainable through other means. This can include witness information, time of occurrence, who made the initial call to law enforcement, and factors such as interactions with the security officer.

Personnel Files: Secure copies of the personnel files of all officers involved. Also, take this opportunity to self-audit your training programs and hiring process. Regardless of whether or not it appears the officers were at fault, evaluate compliance with your internal hiring standards to see if all appropriate steps were taken prior to hire and assignment. Check to see if the proper training was conducted during orientation and on the job training at the site. Also verify that the officer possessed the correct license and that it is current.

Customer Correspondence: Save all emails, letters, and other forms of communication between your company and the customer concerning the incident. Make sure that the insurance company remains aware of any request that are made to you from the customer, or the customer's counsel, such as wanting a claim update or seeking a decision on claim reimbursement. This should include any communication from the customer's insurance company as well.

Depending on the individual situation, other steps may need to be taken and additional considerations explored. There may also be reasons that require steps to be omitted or modified, but the key is making sure you have everything at the initial stage. You may not have a chance later to recreate something that no longer exists.

THE DAY ARRIVES

I can still recall the first time I had the experience of a lawsuit landing on my desk. It was a case involving a fire that had damaged a customer's property a year or so earlier. The attorney bringing the action against us was one of the most well-known figures from the local plaintiffs' bar. I had met him on occasion, but most of my experience was based on seeing his larger-than-life persona on various billboards that dotted the interstate across the state. The mere sight of his name on the summons immediately induced a rush of panic. To complicate matters, it appeared we were being sued by an insurance company – not the customer. Not only was I receiving a crash course on what it felt like to be a civil defendant, I was about to get a rather abrupt education in the concept of subrogation.

Fortunately, I had the foresight to notify the insurance carrier when the fire occurred just in case something happened down the road. Neither the insurance company, nor I, felt that we would ever hear from this matter again and the claim would be filed away as a distant memory. Even the customer, who of course was not thrilled about the fire occurring, did not seem to place any amount of blame on us. So not only was I reeling from the shock of being sued, I was also trying to comprehend how we got in this situation in the first place. While lawsuits have thankfully never become an everyday occurrence in my world, at this early stage in my career all I knew how to do was stare at it and hoped it would somehow go away.

Once I collected my thoughts, I began considering a number of responses to this life-changing document laying in front of me. Should I call the customer and ask them what is going on? Should I call the attorney who filed it and explain that he had somehow made a horrible mistake since we were not the responsible party (after all – I didn't start the fire)? Should I begin to contact local attorneys to represent our company and hopefully comfort me with reassuring words of brilliant legal strategy that would dispose of this nuisance in a matter of days? Fortunately, somewhere deep in my memory and shallow experience I was able to summon enough sense to determine that none of these were great options. Instead, I immediately called my insurance carrier and told them of my predicament and asked them to stand by the fax machine to receive this high-priority document that I was sure would cause them just as much fear and anxiety as it was currently causing me. To my surprise, they did not seem anywhere near as panicked and afraid as I was. In fact, they seemed to have dealt with this type of matter before. Imagine that. As they explained to me the process of retaining counsel to work on our behalf and how they expected the process to unfold, I began the transition from fear to understanding, and ultimately confidence that we would survive this. In the end, the case was dismissed and we never had to face off in court or dig too deep into issues of liability or contract language.

When you are served with lawsuits related to the security services industry, they will typically fall into one of three categories.[5] Let's look at the dynamics of each.

Lawsuits filed directly by victims

The risk associated with lawsuits brought by victims of crime or other losses will in many ways be a direct reflection of the type of business you chose to engage in. Apartments, Shopping Malls, Nightclubs, Hotels, and other properties frequented by the public will almost guarantee your involvement in some type of litigation, if you are in business long enough. Although, there are many examples of cases being filed arising from incidents occurring in

---

[5]Beyond these categories a security company can also expect to be named in litigation related to discrimination or other employment law issues. The categories listed here deal exclusively with liability and contractual matters.

industrial and other nonpublic settings as well. These are sometimes brought by the victim against the security company for lack of having adequate security measures to prevent the crime. It will usually be accompanied by claims of negligent hiring, negligent supervision, negligent training, and failure to properly follow stated policies relating to securing the environment. If you find yourself to be the only defendant, you will be left to defend your company and the actions of your officers. While circumstances can vary substantially from case to case, this can be somewhat difficult. Especially in cases where there is a legitimate victim who has sustained an injury as a result of a painful and often horrific encounter with a perpetrator or even a fellow employee. These lawsuits also tend to attract media coverage depending on the severity of the crime and the willingness of the plaintiff's counsel to use public exposure to influence the outcome. On a few occasions, I have actually received information from the media that our company was being sued – even before I was aware that a suit had been filed.

In order to succeed in these types of actions, you must be very diligent in reconstructing what actually occurred and what the actions were of the security officer before, during, and after the event. It is also very wise to ensure that all officers involved know not to speak with any members of the media, or investigators working on behalf of the plaintiff's attorney. I can recall at least one occasion, where I had spoken to a former employee about an incident only to learn half way through our conversation that he had recently given a wide-ranging interview to a person working on behalf of the plaintiff.[6] My entire focus shifted from "tell me what happened" to "tell me what you told them." It is vitally important to control the flow of information from day one in dealing with this type of case.

The general rule when a negligent security lawsuit is filed is that you will rarely find yourself as the only defendant. This is true for a couple of different reasons. First, it is only logical and expected that your customer will be viewed as the responsible party. They are the identifiable party and will be seen, at least initially, as the entity primarily responsible for making sure their customers and visitors remain safe. Second, it is often necessary to sue the customer to find out who else can be a target. Often times our professional egos guide us to the opinion that everyone knows that we are the security provider for XYZ Incorporated. But do they really know? I have had several cases where the only reason we were added to a case was because

---

[6]Professional Rules of Conduct prohibit attorneys from contacting parties they know are represented by counsel, but the issue of speaking with current or former nonmanagerial employees of a corporate defendant is more complex. In some situations it is acceptable, while not always perceived to be ethical, to contact former or even current officers.

our identity was revealed during the discovery phase of an already pending case. One of my favorite legal anecdotes is from a deposition I was attending after being sued by a crime victim.

The plaintiff had settled the matter with the property owner, our customer, without litigation and had for some reason decided to file an action against us almost a year later. Our outside counsel was taking the victim's deposition and I was observing and contributing questions and advice during breaks. Throughout his deposition the plaintiff never mentioned our company by name, and even appeared to be confused about our relationship with the property owner. In fact, he would often insert the name of our customer when describing what he viewed as a failure to keep him safe. At the final break our counsel asked if I had any other questions that I would like the plaintiff to answer. I told him that in order to satisfy my lingering curiosity, ask him how, when, and why he decided to sue us.

As the session was wrapping up, our counsel obliged my request and asked the plaintiff why after settling with the property owner did he decide many months later to file an action against the security company? He began to tell a story that if I had not been in the room to hear, I am not sure I would accept as nonfiction. The plaintiff described a day almost a year earlier where he was called to testify in the criminal trial of the person who had harmed him. He stated that as he was leaving the courthouse he ran into a family friend who happened to be an attorney. The conversation naturally turned to his ordeal, and as any good attorney would, the friend began to inquire about what civil legal action the plaintiff had taken to make sure he was compensated accordingly. The plaintiff testified that he then explained the settlement he had received from the property owner and how grateful he was to have his medical expenses covered. End of the story? Not quite. Not satisfied with the plaintiff's willingness to move on from the matter, the attorney uttered a question that had brought us all to this point: Why don't you sue the security company? When I received the transcript, I highlighted the next sentence spoken by the plaintiff at the end of that deposition: "I thought to myself, ok, sure." "Until that moment I assumed those security guys were regular employees not contractors."

When you find yourself as a codefendant with your customer, from the outset it can be an awkward situation and one that can be difficult to balance when interests become divided. As we will see later during the delicate process of discovery, maintaining a sense of service and protecting your interest can be an uphill battle. While the customers themselves did not make the decision to haul you into a legal battle, and they are not actively pursuing you for any claimed negligence, there is usually a very real possibility that they may be thinking "I am only in this situation because of you!" I have often said that our customers are our partners and maintaining this goal should not be abandoned just because you are both named in a lawsuit, but certain events can occur that will make it much more difficult to achieve that goal.

If the lawsuit is alleging some type of negligence (don't they all?), then at some point the question will turn to who is the "decider" and who was truly responsible and in control of the security functions. This may put the security company, depending on the facts, in a position to have a decent defense, or at minimum argue that they were somewhat limited in what they could or couldn't do. But does that hurt the customer's case? Are you then pointing the proverbial finger at the customer and shouting "it's their fault!" These can be difficult questions to ask.

In some cases you will be asked to consider a Joint Defense agreement when there is more than one defendant to the same action. This is essentially an understanding that the defendant will exchange confidential communication for the parties' mutual benefit and work together in defending the action. Cooperation among counsel in some actions is necessary and presents strategic advantages to both the security company and the customer. But, when divergent interests among codefendants start to appear, arguments about who is really at fault arise, or indemnity claims become a real possibility, cooperation among codefendants is challenging at best. Good communication and willingness to compromise are critical in pursuing a case where both the company and customer are satisfied and not at each other's throats when the case is over.

Lawsuits filed by our customers

It does not take the wise counsel of a Harvard MBA to figure out that getting sued by our customers is not good for business. But often it is more a function of risk shifting and business strategy than it is a blatant attack on our professionalism or performance. But, regardless of the ultimate motivation, the experience can be one that can leave a lasting mark, good or bad, on the customer relationship. In most situations lawsuits filed directly by customers will be under the umbrella of "failure to indemnify." This essentially means that the customer feels that you had the obligation to provide a defense to a lawsuit, or pay a loss, and you have refused to do so. In reality, the failure to extend coverage to a customer ultimately is in the hands of your insurance company, and they will play a large role in any such action, even occasionally as a defendant. But I have also been asked on many occasions to personally guarantee on the behalf of the company that we would cover expenses and losses, irrespective of what our insurance company decided to do. Not a question you want to be asked more than once if you can help it because there is only two possible answers that you can give, and neither of them are good ones.

The sad fact is that in most cases when you are sued by a customer, it will be a former one. Most companies will not survive a relationship that involves an unresolved dispute that lands you both in court. So there is some solace in the fact that if you face this situation, concerns about retaining a contract will likely not be on the table.

Lawsuits filed by insurance companies (subrogation)

Literally, subrogation means one person or party stands in the place of another. Subrogation issues surface when a person has been injured and someone other than the party at fault pays for all or some of the damages resulting from the injury. The party at fault, in the mind of the insurance company, is often the security service provider who failed to prevent the loss. By definition, a subrogation claim allows the insurance company, often the carrier who provides coverage to your customer, to stand in the shoes of the injured party and seek to recover any loss from the real party who caused the loss.

This real-world example may give some clarity on how the issues of subrogation can creep in and cause the security company to be lulled into a false sense of complacency. A local security company was hired to perform patrol rounds at a warehouse that had recently become vacant when the customer ceased operations at the location. However, the building still housed costly equipment, desirable elements such as cooper, and other items that needed to be protected from theft. The officer's duties were clear: make continual foot patrols to ensure you are acting as a deterrent and report any unusual activity or criminal acts to law enforcement immediately.

The warehouse facility was approximately 250,000 square feet and sat on a 15-acre property. One night at approximately 1:00 am the officer on duty was performing his foot patrol on the north end of the warehouse. At the same time, an unknown number of burglars gained access to the warehouse through a rear dock door located on the south end of the warehouse. The property was not equipped with any type of alarm. Valuable equipment was removed, a large amount of cooper was stolen, and part of the property was vandalized. The total loss was over $250,000. According to his report, the officer on duty did not hear the perpetrators enter the warehouse and he did not discover the theft until he made his round at the rear of the building 45 min later.

Obviously this was a bad day for the customer and the security company. But after a full review of the facts, there did not seem to be a real push to hold the security company accountable, and the customer was even somewhat apologetic for not investing in an additional officer or a patrol vehicle for a property of that size. In the end the whole episode was viewed as a wakeup call for the customer who implemented more stringent security measures and continued to use the services of the same security company. The security company never notified their insurance carrier and a report was given to upper management that there was no reason to be concerned since the customer had no intentions of holding them responsible for the theft.

But what the security company did not know was that the customer had initiated the filing of an insurance claim with their carrier. After a lengthy claim process, which did not involve contacting the security company, or amazingly even speaking to the officer, a large sum was paid to the customer to reimburse them for the loss of equipment and damage. The insurance company then turned their attention to finding out who was really to blame for the loss, and to start the process of "standing in the shoes" of the customer in order to seek reimbursement for the claim they had already paid. The logical party was of course the security company.

The process was initiated, as it usually is, by sending a letter to the security company informing that they were exploring who was at fault in relation to the loss suffered by the customer. After some back and forth, and the security company finally making their insurance carrier aware of the matter, there was a decision made by the security company's insurance company that the security provider was not responsible and would not be reimbursing the customer's carrier for the loss. Litigation ensued and the facts of the case were critical to prove or disprove the security company's liability.

Just as would be the case if the action was filed directly by the customer, the central issues in the case were very familiar:

- Was the officer properly performing his duties before, during, and after the theft?
- Was the assignment of a sole officer adequate for the size of the property, and did the security company advise the customer on the proper measures that should be taken to ensure a safe and secure environment?
- Should the officer have noticed the perpetrators on the property, or at minimum, should he have heard the activity?
- Is it reasonable to assume that if the officer would've been performing continual rounds he would've discovered the burglary in process due to the amount of time that would have been required to remove the equipment and cause the property damage?
- Why did it take the officer 45 min to return to the South end of the property?

These were the questions that had to be answered in order for the security company to successfully defend the subrogation action. As you might imagine, the questions can often be difficult to completely address, and answers do not always come quickly. The company was further handicapped by the fact that they did not make an immediate investigation and contact their insurance company from the outset.

Don't get blindsided by a subrogation action. Even though the customer is not holding you responsible, someone, somewhere, may be planning to.

EDUCATING YOUR ATTORNEY

Someone once told me shortly after I expressed my desire to become an attorney that I should only consider this career path if I had no family, neighbors, or friends. Otherwise I was destined to live a life filled with endless pleas for help, late night calls for free legal advice, and I would also be expected to know anything and everything about every law in existence. While that was an obvious exaggeration, I can tell you that this admonition has come to mind many times over the years. There is something very unique that happens to people when they learn that you are an attorney. Many questions naturally start or begin with "is it legal to …." I have also been met with the occasional look of disbelief when I have to confess that I'm not familiar with that particular area of law, or a specific regulation that I have never heard of. I can almost hear them say "excuse me! I thought you were a lawyer" as disappointment comes over their face. But here's some inside information, and a very poorly guarded secret, that most nonattorneys may find surprising: lawyers don't know everything. In fact I have always been particularly frightened of the ones who claim that they do.

Of course this has nothing to do with intellect, training, or even legal experience. It is simply a function of how much or how little an attorney has been exposed to during his or her career. I'm always happy to admit that my legal experience has been mostly contained to the business world, and more specifically in the area of contract security. If someone wants to discuss legal theory and strategy concerning employment law or negligent security, I am more than willing to engage. If you want to discuss the best way to comply with certain provisions of the tax code, or the latest developments in the area of patent law, you have the wrong guy.

While perceptions of attorneys and other professionals are pretty well ingrained in the national psyche, sometimes these assumptions can lead to trouble. I have experienced many occasions in the aftermath of a major incident where I am handed a few basic facts and expected to go fix it. It is almost as if the baton is being passed from one universe to other and from this point on never the two shall meet again. The attorney is expected to enter the legal world and do what he or she needs to be with minimum disruption to the affected parties. I've heard this from numerous colleagues and attorney friends, and I have seen firsthand the danger this can present when working with outside counsel.

It is a safe assumption that most security companies do not have the benefit of having an attorney on staff that is well versed in all aspects of the security industry, and how the business operations and legal aspects should coexist. In fact, even if you have the luxury of an in-house counsel it is a rare occurrence that he or she will directly represent the company in litigation. Therefore, a knowledge base as it relates to our industry is critical when forging a relationship with an outside counsel.

Let me be clear before we go any further, if I am meeting with a new outside counsel who has been litigating for 20+ years and has been retained to represent our interest in a particular matter, no one, including myself, would argue that I am the smartest person in that room. And make no mistake, I am not a client that feels that it is his sole purpose to second-guess every aspect of the counsel's advice, or to make sure that I am in control of every aspect of the case from beginning to end. If I am working with a counsel whose abilities I am confident in, I believe it is my job to let he or she do theirs. But, how much they know about contract security? Are they familiar with the typical bidding process? Are they going to assume that all officers should carry weapons and the ones that don't aren't very effective? Do they know that price considerations are at the very center of virtually all customer relationships in our industry and can certainly have an impact on what measures can be implemented, and what staff can be assigned? This knowledge is not always inherent, even with an outside counsel who has handled security cases before.

Several years ago, I was hired as an expert witness to testify for the plaintiff in a nightclub shooting case where there was obvious gross negligence on the part of the proprietary armed security officers, who could more accurately be described as undercover bouncers carrying semiautomatic weapons. The attorney that I was working for was an individual whom I have a great amount of respect for and who is known throughout the legal community as an excellent litigator and brilliant mind. I assumed that he was hiring me as more of a necessity to have a mechanism to introduce the damning evidence that he had already accumulated against the establishment. But I quickly learned that despite his legal brilliance and wealth of courtroom talent, his perception of the private security industry was quite flawed. For example, he made no real distinction between a nightclub bouncer and a uniformed security officer stationed at an industrial facility. I also quickly realized that his overall view of our industry, and its inherent worth, was not very high. Of course in hindsight this was to be expected because he had just spent the last 6 months working on a case where the so-called security professionals were nothing more than regular bar patrons who were given a few bucks to make sure nothing got out of hand.

I feel it is part of my responsibility and mission to make sure that any outside counsel representing our interests not only has a firm grasp on the facts of the case, but also understands the entire business environment and what specific aspects can greatly impact the legal procedure. I never take for granted that the attorney I am working with has a full and clear picture of how the contract security industry operates. At this point, it should come as no shock that perceptions of our industry often trend toward the negative. This can be true even with the legal professionals that we work with. An article written a few years ago even pointed out how the evolution from the label of security "guard" to security "officer" was important in changing perceptions about the professionalism and value our employees exhibit each day.[7] Don't overlook the need to educate your attorneys on what we actually do.

Equally as important as educating outside attorneys on the value of our services, is making sure they understand the overall concept of how our business works. Most, if not all, attorneys that you work with will have frequent contact with security officers. This may be greeting the lobby officer when they arrive to work each day, or being screened by security personnel during frequent trips to the courthouse. However, few may realize what goes on behind the scenes.

To ensure that there is a comprehensive understanding from the start of our relationship, I follow a similar script when orientating attorneys to our company and our industry:

- Brief History of Your Company: Include ownership, number of employees, office and service area locations, and customer base served.
- Brief description of security officer industry in general.
- State and our local licensing regulations regarding security officers. Also provide information concerning required training and background checks that all officers must go through.
- Internal company policies on hiring and ongoing training.

In addition to a general discussion concerning your company and industry, I also use the first meeting with an outside counsel to establish key pieces of

---

[7]Security Officers: *How Changing Titles Changes Perceptions* by Douglas Fogwell, October 2012 http://www.securitymagazine.com/articles/83657-security-officers-how-changing-titles-changes-perceptions

information about the incident that gave rise to the lawsuit. The following factors should be discussed or presented at the earliest stage:

- Brief history of the contractual relationship between the security company and customer. This should include any and all security assessments or recommendations that may have been provided by the security company over the life of the contract.
- Information concerning any similar prior incidents at the location in question.
- Personnel files of the officers involved, highlighting any prior disciplinary or background issues.
- A description of the training provided to the officers involved, as well as documented training records.
- Written post instructions for the location in question, or if unavailable, a description of what duties were expected to be performed.
- All current contractual agreements between the customer and the security company.
- Any and all other documents relevant to the action such as daily activity reports, incident reports, statements, and witness information.

Based on my experience, you will not get many opportunities to have meaningful one-on-one discussions with outside counsel, so you have to make each one count. Small talk is great, but through proper organization you can greatly improve the chances of a strong and competent defense. Never be afraid to question their understanding of certain aspects of our business, and don't shy away from opportunities to cement their ability to grasp all the nuances of the contract security relationship. Not only will they not be offended, the best attorneys are the ones who know what their limitations are and how to address them. You may not get a second chance if you allow the "he must know that" line of thinking to invade your thoughts.

The life of a lawsuit begins with the initial complaint being filed and delivered, but unfortunately that is only the beginning of an often long and painful journey that can exact a great financial and emotional cost. The key, once again, is to be prepared with knowledge and to have a plan of action. When teaching human resource professionals and management employees about the proper way to discipline and terminate an employee, I often say that if anyone acts surprised when you are terminating them, you may not be doing your job as a supervisor correctly. The same goes for lawsuits. If you have a plan and process in place well before the day arrives, you will not only be free from shock when it hits your desk, you will be ready to spring into action and begin the process of fighting back. And as we are about to see, the road does not get any easier from here.

The adventure of discovery for a contract security company

To state the obvious, litigation is expensive. That is the main driving factor behind the reason that many cases settle well before reaching the inside of a courtroom. Many law students dream of spending their days arguing with judges and juries only to learn that the life of a typical lawyer consists of more negotiation and preparation than it does litigation. For all case types, a trial is the single most time-intensive stage of litigation, encompassing between one-third and one-half of total litigation time in cases that progress all the way through to trial. The median costs of a premises liability trial is around $55,000, and could go much higher depending on the issues involved.[1] The discovery phase of trial is often the most expensive element of the entire process. This is where the case is often won or lost, and when decisions are made on future strategies.

Discovery can become a very complicated task and definitely warrants the assistance of an attorney. The discovery process can often be frustrating and disheartening. It will force security companies to examine where the strengths, and unfortunately where many weaknesses, are present in their processes and overall business model. I've always found that while discovery can be a daunting process, it is also a very important element for both sides in order to know where you stand and where the case is likely to head. Early in my career, I became somewhat cynical and jaded concerning the formalities of litigation, including discovery, because I assumed that at some point the insurance company would likely just settle, rendering the hours I spent compiling documents and answering questions virtually meaningless and ultimately inconsequential in the grand scheme. But I have since learned that the discovery phase of a case is one of, if not the, most compelling

---

[1]*Estimating the Cost of Civil Litigation* (January 2013)
Paula Hannaford-Agor, Director, Center for Jury Studies
Nicole L. Waters, Principal Court Research Consultant
http://www.courtstatistics.org/~/media/microsites/files/csp/data%20pdf/csph_online2.ashx

and influential factors heading into any settlement discussions. By knowing where you are strong, and where you are vulnerable, you can begin to paint a picture of what is likely to occur if a trial becomes a reality.

Discovery is also another legal process where the attorney cannot simply take over and do it all. The security company will have to invest time and resources to make sure that the responses are timely and accurate, and all the information is sufficiently addressed. Without prior experience, engaging in the discovery process can be very intimidating and, at times, overwhelming. We all have likely heard stories of litigants whose sole strategy may be to bury the other side in a mountain of discovery requests with the hope that the other side will wave the white flag and give into any demands on the table. Here again, knowledge is the key, and making sure that everyone is educated on the process will pay off throughout the struggle of discovery.

Discovery is essentially the pretrial phase in a lawsuit in which each party investigates the facts of a case, through the rules of civil procedure, by obtaining evidence from the opposing party and others by means of discovery devices, including requests for answers to interrogatories, requests for production of documents, requests for admissions, and depositions. As the name denotes, each party is attempting to "discover" certain things about the incident and it is not uncommon for lawsuits to be filed without knowing some key facts prior to the discovery phase. This is why some lawsuits will be served with initial discovery requests attached from the outset. Many times, parties to lawsuits are added or removed based on the information uncovered in the discovery phase.

Under the laws of individual states, civil discovery is typically broadly defined and parties to a civil action are allowed to ask for virtually any material, which is "reasonably calculated to lead to the discovery of admissible evidence."[2] This is a much broader standard than simply restricting discovery to only finding relevant evidence because it allows for the party to acquire materials and testimony that may not necessarily be used as direct evidence, but it could lead to the discovery of other evidence that would be relevant. I have been asked by supervisors and subordinates during discovery phases if we "really have to turn this or that over to the other side"? The quickest and simplest answer is that if the only reason not to do so is because it would hurt our case, then yes we have to. However, discovery is not without limits. Certain types of information are generally protected from discovery, including information which is privileged such

---

[2]This qualifying language, or similar phrasing, is found in many state rules of civil procedure and is the key concept behind the proposition that discovery efforts should be guided by the notion that it will ultimately *lead* to admissible evidence.

as attorney–client communications, and the information prepared in anticipation of the litigation.

But before we go any further in our discussion about the discovery process, let me hammer a very important point home at the outset. Nothing can hinder the discovery process more than not properly preserving documents and other forms of information. The duty to preserve evidence may arise before – and certainly arises without – a preservation letter sent by the opposing party. In fact, the duty can arise long before. A party's obligation to preserve the evidence is generally held to arise when the party knows, or has a reason to know, that the evidence may be relevant to future litigation. This "reasonable anticipation of litigation" standard means that any person or company who should see a claim or lawsuit on the horizon must act, even before a preservation letter or lawsuit has materialized, to cease the activities which are likely to destroy electronic or tangible evidence and must take affirmative steps to preserve such evidence. Often the span of time between the actual event and eventual litigation can sometimes occur over a number of years, and while we have already explored the need for gathering and organizing various forms of information when incidents occur, a more formal process is often necessary. The issuance of what is referred to as a "litigation hold," often comes in the form of a written request from a variety of different parties. A litigation hold letter can be sent to the security company by the counsel representing the victim, your customer, or even your own outside counsel. These notifications serve as a formal reminder and instruction to maintain any and all forms of information relating to the event in question. But there is no reason, in fact that there are practical considerations on the contrary, to wait until you receive this letter to begin the process of making sure that no evidence is disposed off prematurely.

Prior to the litigation being filed, and certainly well in advance of outside counsel being retained, I will send out an internal communication to either our local branch office, or even in some cases a specific site, outlining the expectations to preserve any current and future documents and information relating to a specific incident.[3] I include with this the instruction to forward any newly discovered material that may become available at a later date. I have been involved in many cases where a document, a series of emails, or a random file did not seem to be significant at the time of the occurrence, but became hugely important in a future action. Unfortunately, in some of those cases, the files had since disappeared or had been disposed of, and in other cases I learned after the fact that vital documents existed without my knowledge.

---

[3]A sample internal "litigation hold" letter is included as Appendix D.

I received an unexpected phone call one morning from a veteran salesperson. He asked me about the status of a particular case, that I had been working on for some time, involving a theft at a customer facility. After some small talk about the litigation, he asked if he needed to keep a copy of his sales notes from the time when the service had originally commenced. When I began to ask for a description of the so-called notes, I learned that they contained nothing short of a full-blown security assessment including communicated recommendations. They were certainly vital pieces of information that could be used to our benefit in the pending action. Why did I not have it before that day? Simple: I never asked. From that day forward, I make sure that any potential impacted internal parties are included and receive the litigation hold notification. This will prevent any embarrassment, or even more worrisome legal sanctions, that can come later when you are unable to produce documents because they were not preserved properly.

It is also important to never make assumptions or take things for granted when it comes to preserving documents and evidence. Your notifications may need to include third-party vendors such as information technology partners and companies providing electronic officer tour recording data. If at this point you are thinking that no one can be faulted for simply not having something, or that the plaintiff will accept at face value your claim that certain things do not exist, when you make it to the witness stand you may find this assumption is extremely flawed. My first real experience as a witness in a big-time case came in an action where we were being sued because an elderly patron was robbed in the parking lot of a retail establishment. After hours upon hours of preparation, I felt as though I was ready to face any questions that may come from the other side. However, I was not prepared to endure a string of questions that must've lasted at least 30 min concerning our policy and procedures for maintaining accurate business records. The facts of the case quickly took a backseat to the issue of whether or not we had fully disclosed all the materials requested of us in the discovery phase. I'm thankful no video evidence exists of that episode because I'm quite confident that my responses were less than satisfactory, and likely had our attorney second-guessing his choice of a corporate representative to put on the stand.

Now let's look at the discovery process in general, and its unique application in security cases.

TYPES OF DISCOVERY
Requests for admissions

Just as the name implies, requests for admissions ask the security company to admit or deny certain carefully worded questions. For example, you may be asked by the plaintiff to admit certain specific facts related to an incident for the purpose of attempting to prove your liability. Since the parties are asked to admit or deny allegations in the original document that starts a lawsuit, usually referred to as the complaint, requests for admissions may seem futile and repetitive. But, when properly used, they allow a party to dig deeper into issues beyond those required to state a cause of action, such that certain reasonable inferences can be drawn as a result of the answers obtained. Request for admission can also be used at depositions to "remind" the party testifying of their previous answers.

Responses to request for admission should be carefully considered, but at the early stage of litigation a party may reasonably assert that they do not have enough information to admit or deny what is being asked. And often, the questions are so slanted toward the plaintiff's ultimate legal theory, there is no choice but to deny rather than make an admission that would serve as a stipulation that everything the injured party is alleging is correct.

In the hypothetical case of Smith v. ABC Security Company and Litigation Lane Apartments, a typical request for admissions would look similar to the following:[4]

1. Admit that for all time periods relevant to the complaint filed in this matter, ABC Security Company was an enterprise engaged in providing security services for the purpose of deterring, preventing, and responding to criminal activity.
2. Admit that the plaintiff was a tenant of Litigation Lane Apartments.
3. Admit that ABC Security had a duty and obligation to protect the property, on and around Litigation Lane, from criminal activity.
4. Admit that ABC Company entered into an agreement with Litigation Lane Apartments to provide security services and protect the residents from criminal activity.
5. Admit that the "agreement" signed in December 2014, between ABC Security Company and Litigation Lane Apartments mandated that ABC Security only assign officers that are "well-trained" and "well-qualified" to the property.
6. Admit that Officer Joe Jones was assigned to the property on January 1, 2015.

---

[4]An example is provided for each discovery device. Each example was constructed by using standard requests taken from actual cases to illustrate what to except in regard to documents sought, interrogatories posed, etc. Depending on the case at hand, more, less, or different information may be sought.

7. Admit that Officer Joe Jones' duties on the night of January 1, 2015 were, in part, to keep all unauthorized parties, including criminal trespassers, from entering Litigation Lane Property.
8. Admit that Officer Joe Jones failed to receive any training in the area of deterring, detecting, and responding to criminal activity.
9. Admit that Officer Joe Jones failed to deter or detect the presence of the trespasser who attacked and injured the plaintiff on the night of January 1, 2015.
10. Admit that Officer Joe Jones did not notify any law enforcement agency or respond to any pleas for help after the plaintiff was injured by an unknown assailant on January 1, 2015.

Request for admissions are asking you (the defendant) to admit or deny the truth of these statements under oath. If admitted, the statement is considered to be true for all purposes in the pending case. Requests for admission are sometimes used toward the end of the discovery process to settle uncontested issues and simplify the trial, but I have also seen them used early on in an attempt to get a defendant "on the record" about certain matters. I have seen my responses to request for admissions used in depositions many months later in an attempt to challenge one of my answers, or indicate that later evidence points out that something should have been "admitted" rather than "denied."

Interrogatories

Unlike requests for admissions, interrogatories ask open-ended questions. For example, a security company may be asked to identify all the evidence upon which they intend to rely in support of their claims or defenses. Interrogatories can often become quite complex with multiple subparts, so most states limit the number of interrogatories that either party can ask the other (the limit is 25 under the Federal rules). The use of interrogatories will be governed by the law where the case has been filed.

If you are in litigation, it is quite likely that you will receive a set of interrogatories to which you must respond. The first thing to know about interrogatory responses is that your responses will, in most cases, be verified. Verification is essentially just an affidavit in which the responding party swears under oath that the responses to the interrogatories are true.

Responding to interrogatories typically means nothing more or less than reading the question and writing out an answer. But the real problem that arises is how much time, effort, and research is put into responding to a particular interrogatory. The interrogatory may ask you to provide a vast amount of information related to a number of different areas. Exactly how much detail and how much work to do in responding to an interrogatory should be the subject of some discussion between you and the counsel.

Typical interrogatories can range from the simple and direct (state your name), to overwhelmingly complex (provide the name and contact information of every crime victim who was injured on a premises you serviced in the last 5 years). Many attorneys use standard interrogatory forms customized for the type of case at hand, so you can also expect to see some questions that may not have any relevance to the proceedings.

The following example is a good representation of what to expect when receiving a list of interrogatories:

1. Please identify yourself by stating your full name, present address, date and place of birth, Social Security number, and the name of your spouse.
2. Please state the name and address of any potential party to this lawsuit, not already named as a party hereto.
3. Please state how your business relationship with Litigation Lane Apartments began and on what date. If there is a contract, or any other document memorializing this relationship, please provide a copy.
4. Please state whether or not you are aware of the policy against allowing any nonresidents to gain access to Litigation Lane Apartments property. If your answer is in the affirmative, please state fully what this policy was.
5. Please describe in detail what services you provide as it pertains to crime prevention services as advertised on your website. Please also list dates, times, and attendance rosters for any crime prevention classes you held during the time you were providing services to Litigation Lane Apartments.
6. Please describe in detail any security evaluations, risk assessments, crime analysis, or any other study you undertook before or during the time you provided security services to Litigation Lane Apartments. Please include any recommended security measures that were provided to Litigation Lane Apartments prior to you commencing security services.
7. Please list all of the professional organizations ABC Security Company holds membership in. Please also list any certifications or other professional designations.
8. Please provide a copy of all marketing material, standard proposals, or other advertising related to your crime prevention services.
9. Please provide a list of all customers over the 5 years immediately preceding the vicious attack on the plaintiff that occurred on

January 1, 2015, whereby any type of workplace violence or violent criminal activity occurred. Please include in your response the name of the customer, address, type of criminal or violent incident, and the date of such incident.

10. Please state whether or not there was any video surveillance at the south end of Litigation Lane Apartments on January 1, 2015. If so, please state whether or not you are in custody and control of said video, or if you have knowledge of who would be in custody and control of said video.

11. Please state the name, position, and current employment status of each and every person employed by ABC Security who was working at Litigation Lane Apartments for the 6-month period immediately preceding the vicious attack on the plaintiff that occurred on January 1, 2015.

12. Please describe in detail your internal hiring process including recruitment, screening, and training.

13. Please describe in detail how ABC Security Company was first notified of the vicious attack suffered by the plaintiff on January 1, 2015.

14. Please provide a detailed listing of any and all criminal activity observed and/or reported by the employees of ABC Security Company that occurred on or around the property known as Litigation Lane Apartments for the 6-month period immediately preceding the vicious attack on the plaintiff that occurred on January 1, 2015.

15. Please state the name of each and every insurance company that may be liable to satisfy, indemnify, or reimburse all or part of the judgment that may ultimately be entered in this action. Please state the dollar amount of any and all liability insurance coverage available in this action.

As with requests for admission, you can see that answering the interrogatories can be a delicate process as well to ensure that you are not moving the case in the wrong direction. Sometimes, rather than answering the interrogatory, you (or your attorney) may wish to object to the request on legal grounds. Common objections that can be raised may relate to the fact that the question is phrased in compound form requiring you to answer more than one inquiry at a time. Another likely objection will be that the question is vague, ambiguous, or unintelligible. Sometimes it is just not possible to comprehend what the other side is asking. With many interrogatories, the request is not reasonably calculated to lead to the discovery of relevant, admissible evidence. All interrogatories must be relevant to the issues in the case. If a request does not likely lead to the discovery of relevant, admissible evidence, you can object. Attorneys will often use this standard objection to stop any "fishing expedition" for the sole purpose of getting information the other side may not otherwise be entitled to.

Interrogatories should be taken seriously, and although you will hopefully have the assistance of a competent attorney guiding you, the ultimate responsibility for answering truthfully and accurately rests with you. Some simple tips can assist in this effort. Review each request to ensure that you fully understand the question, and can answer it completely. Be sure to review all the information, documents, and other evidence available to you before answering to ensure that your responses are accurate and thorough. If you feel that you do not have adequate information or knowledge, and there is no one else in the organization who does, do not hesitate to inform your counsel that you cannot respond. I have seen many attempts to create a clever answer, or make the answer longer than it should be, simply because they do not feel that they have any real information to provide. This is of course unwise for many different reasons, and sometimes the best answer is "I don't know."

You should also complete your responses to the interrogatories in the order in which they are laid out in the document. This may seem to be a minor point, but I can tell you firsthand that attorneys will be very appreciative of the fact that they are receiving draft responses that are easily organized and identifiable to the original request.

Request for production

Arguably one of the most useful tools for discovery, requests for production allows the plaintiff to ask the security company to provide documents, or other evidence, in an effort to build their case. This is the process used to actually obtain most of the real evidence that the parties will rely on when they move toward trial. Requests for production can also be directed to nonparties and obtained through a subpoena. In more complex cases, documents and things that are responsive to requests for production can be immense, filling entire warehouses, and this procedure can often become a very expensive element of many cases.

The responding party is basically required to furnish copies of any documents that are responsive to the request, except for those that are legally privileged. The responding party can also submit a response to the other party explaining why the documents cannot be produced. For example, when the documents have been destroyed, or would be unduly burdensome to produce, or they are simply not in your possession. However, the plaintiff then may file a Motion to Compel Discovery to obtain the documents.

Let's continue with our hypothetical case and see what a typical request for the production of documents might look like:

1. Please provide a copy of any and all marketing brochures related to ABC Security Company's services.
2. Please provide a complete copy of any material, whatsoever, utilized in your crime prevention workshops, including but not limited to, handouts, research documents, PowerPoint presentations, and photographs.
3. Please provide a complete copy of any and all reports, statements, and any other written material relating to the vicious attack on the plaintiff, which occurred on January 1, 2015.
4. Please provide a complete copy of all written correspondence between ABC Security Company and Litigation Lane Apartments for the last 5 years.
5. Please provide a complete copy of any contractual agreement in effect as of January 1, 2015.
6. Please provide a complete copy of the personnel file of all ABC Security Company employees who were assigned to Litigation Lane Apartments on January 1, 2015, and the 6-month timeframe proceeding January 1, 2015.
7. Please provide a complete copy of any and all training materials used to train ABC Security Company employees who were assigned to Litigation Lane Apartments.
8. Please provide a complete copy of any internal incident reports, daily activity reports, or any other written documents pertaining to criminal activity occurring at Litigation Lane Apartments for the 6-month period preceding January 1, 2015.
9. Please provide a complete copy of any photographs, video, or audio recording that is in your possession of the vicious attack on the plaintiff on January 1, 2015.
10. Please provide a complete copy of all the insurance policies insuring ABC Security Company that were in effect on January 1, 2015.

When utilizing a request for production, the plaintiff is seeking to obtain all the records relating to the customer location and its security operations. It is their goal to establish, as early as possible in the process, that the defendant did not act in a reasonable and prudent manner while designing or implementing the security measures. Through document requests they hope to show that the security company knew of prior problems at the location (foreseeability), did not follow normal industry standards (negligence), had no real concern for the safety of the employees, visitors, or residents (Profit v. People), and did not offer any real or different solutions to obvious problems (Status Quo). The documents provided in the request for production will, in all likelihood, be used as exhibits in depositions and ultimately at trial. It may sound like an obvious piece of advice, but do not neglect to keep a copy of every single page of the documentation that is turned over to the plaintiff. Do not neglect to read each document and have a thorough understanding of what is contained in every one. This is another area where you cannot simply let the attorney do all the work. If you are the one sitting for the deposition, and you fail to have a thorough understanding of all documents now in the possession of the plaintiff, it will have a negative impact on your testimony.

Depositions

Depositions are the process of taking live testimony from witnesses and parties *before* a trial. The witness or party is required to appear and testify under oath before a court reporter who records the entire proceeding. These proceedings are usually done in an attorney's office with representatives of both or all of the parties in attendance. In cases involving a security company, where your customer is a codefendant, you will have the added pressure of possibly having your customer in the room with you during your testimony. In most civil cases, a corporate representative will be asked to give a deposition on behalf of the party. In the case of a security company, this may be an in-house counsel, a high-level executive, or another member of the management. This is the person who will speak about the overall general policy and procedures of the company, and will also have some knowledge of the facts of the case. In addition, fact witnesses such as the management employees who service the account, or the officers who were working during the incident, will also likely give depositions in most cases. While the testimony and questioning in depositions are governed by the usual rules of evidence, with no judge present to rule on any objections, any protestations are usually just recorded by the court reporter and dealt with later if the testimony is introduced at trial. So essentially, the witness is on their own.

Preparation is vitally important leading up to a deposition as the given can have a tremendous impact on the case. Unfortunately, the media has done a good job portraying witness testimony in movies and on TV, so most witnesses may expect the deposition to be filled with bombshells and refusals to answer. The reality is much tamer, but it can still be an intense environment, especially when bad facts are lurking.

I take my role as a general counsel very seriously and feel that I have an obligation to guide our employees through whatever legal process they may find themselves in. I have prepared many managers, security officers, and other employees to be deposed in various situations over the years. Through trial and error, I have learned what preparation techniques are effective, and which ones can be detrimental. One of the things that I always point out is that the facts will be the same when you walk out of the deposition, as they were when you walked in. If the facts are in your favor, the deposition will go smoothly, but if they aren't, many times all you can do is hold on and try to survive the ride.

As I began to prepare a veteran manager to be deposed in a case involving a workplace shooting, he volunteered that he had never testified in court or given a deposition before. He seemed extremely nervous and asked many questions about the process and what to expect. I gave him my standard deposition advice and also assured him that no matter what occurred during the session, I could guarantee that he would live through it. But, unfortunately, there were a few issues that we both knew were going to be front and center during the deposition, and it was fairly certain that the plaintiff would hit them early and often. At the conclusion of our meeting, a couple of days before the scheduled deposition, he asked me to give him a list of tips or techniques on how to avoid the hard-hitting questions he knew would be forthcoming. I not only explained to him once again the proper way to conduct himself in the deposition, but also had no real choice but to bluntly tell him that there was no real escape from the facts and all he can do is make the other side do their job and put in the work to get the information they sought.

During his deposition a couple of days later, there were several different times when he turned to me and gave me a pained expression that seem to cry out for help. At the first break, somewhat exasperated, he asked me" isn't there something you can do to stop this?" I did not have any great words of comfort or quick tips and tricks to stop the tenacious line of questioning. Sometimes, when you have bad facts, you have to endure bad depositions.

There are some key things to remember about depositions. What really counts is your live testimony at trial. That is what the judge and jury will hear. Generally, your deposition will not be used at trial unless it contradicts what you say on the witness stand. But what you say in depositions can alter the course of the plaintiff's strategy. This means that nothing you say at the deposition can typically help your side's case, but it can hurt. Don't go into the deposition thinking you have any chance to change the mind of the opposing party. I have given many depositions, some good some bad, and even when I have felt like I have taken every question and turned it to our ultimate advantage, I did not receive an apology from the plaintiff or promise to dismiss the case as soon as possible. They are not looking for reasons why their case should not go forward, they're looking for you to give them ways to make it stronger.

I have been given several practical tips on surviving depositions that are universal and effective. While every session is unique, following these proven steps can assist greatly in improving your deposition performance.

Always tell the truth – this may seem obvious, and you may find it insulting for someone to suggest that you would do otherwise. However, this advice is not offered to anyone who is contemplating being dishonest. Let's face it, if they're willing to think about lying, someone telling them not to is not going to do much to sway them. This is for those individuals who may consciously, or subconsciously, add or remove facts because they feel the actual answer is not appropriate or comprehensive enough. I've seen this quite often when witnesses are asked about specific dates. I'm always amazed when witnesses quote exact dates and times when asked during depositions. Sometimes I will find out later that they were merely agreeing with the attorney for fear of looking foolish for not knowing, thereby turning an estimation into a purported fact rather than simply admitting they did not know.

Listen to the question – most witnesses are filled with anxiety and nerves. And because they have often been over prepared with aggressive techniques and the goal of anticipating every line of inquiry, the witnesses are almost preprogrammed to expect certain questions. This can result in the witness actually answering the question before it is even asked. During my preparation of witnesses, I often tell them that I can reasonably anticipate some of the questions that are going to be asked, but there are a multitude of others that I may not know are coming. One of the best pieces of advice I was given for my deposition was to keep your mouth shut until the attorney finishes with the question and make sure that you understand it before you start your answer. There have been many times that I was certain that I would be asked a series of questions that never came up. I am sometimes strangely disappointed that I will not get to use the information I have prepared, but I have learned that if they don't ask, I don't answer.

Make certain that you understand the question being asked – there is a natural tendency for witness to want to avoid looking as if they are unqualified to be there. This can result in a witness attempting to answer questions they think they were asked, as opposed to the ones that are actually being presented. I must confess that in my younger days, I would give plaintiff attorneys fits by pouncing on any perceived flaws in their wording or improper phrasing used to offer a question that I fully understood, but was not technically accurate. I considered it my chief goal to make the other side ask me the right question before I would grace them with my answer. But, my attempts to be evasive aside, there are oftentimes when there are genuine misunderstandings about the questions that are asked. Witnesses should never be intimidated to the point where they feel they cannot ask for a question to be clarified before answering.

Most plaintiff attorneys will even be appreciative that you are taking the time to point out that there may be some confusion about what's being asked.

Answer only the question you are asked – there's probably nothing that the plaintiff's attorney likes more than a witness who gives long and detailed answers in depositions. In my estimation, there are two extremes of witnesses. (1) Those who give almost exclusively "yes" and "no" answers and refuse to expound on any particular topic and (2) those who give 20 min speeches regardless of how simple the inquiry is. I was preparing a security officer for a deposition related to a crime that had occurred at a customer facility. I had told the officer that at some point he should be prepared to explain his many years of experience in the security industry and the numerous training classes he had attended during his career. When the time for his deposition arrived he was ready to perform. He was asked to state his name and his response not only included that information but also a 5-min recitation of his security officer experience and training classes that he had attended. The plaintiff's attorney had to ask him to stop talking so that he could ask the second question – which was "what is your current address?"

Use plain, simple language – this may come as a revelation, but most attorneys taking your deposition, and certainly others that may hear or read it later, are not well-versed in all matters relating to private security. Ignorance of this fact can cause the witness to inadvertently speak in industry lingo and use words and phrases that are difficult to understand. I have been stopped many times and asked to explain what I meant by certain phrases or words because I was the only person in the room who knew what "I" was talking about. Security professionals and witnesses in general can also fall into the trap of thinking that the more elevated the language, the more effective the testimony will be; this is rarely true. Remember, even though depositions are not routinely seen by juries or judges, they can be. Assume that your audience knows nothing about your industry and your experiences. Instead of saying that you recommended the "additional deployment of a non-lethal uniformed security countermeasure," it will make the day much shorter to simply explain that you proposed to the customer that another unarmed security officer be placed on the property.

Take your time – in depositions, and even more so at trial, a minute can feel like an eternity. Witnesses can be made to feel the answers should be given immediately without any delay. Add the ominous presence of video camera a few feet from your face, and this can cause the average person to feel that they must spit out a quick answer in order to appear responsive. But there is nothing wrong with taking a couple of moments to consider an answer that may not be subject to immediate recall. When dealing with documents, don't hesitate to ask to take another look, or to be given a minute to read. I have come to expect that plaintiff's attorneys will offer me a large contract or a series of documents and then immediately ask me a very pointed question about its contents. If I know the answer immediately, great. But often I will respectfully ask for at least a couple of minutes to actually read the document. This is usually the case when I am asked questions that start with the proposition of "it doesn't say that anywhere in there does it?" Take your time, trust me, they will wait.

Do not take guesses – witnesses in depositions can sometimes feel as if they are required to be preprogrammed robots who must have a succinct answer for every question posed. Otherwise, why are they there? It is actually okay not to remember something, or not to recall minute details about a very specific date, time, or even an event. Now, I am not talking about the stereotypical image of the shadowy political figure who is hauled before a congressional committee and answers 90% of the Senator's questions with "I don't recall," but rather those times in depositions where you're being pressed for a specific answer and you frankly don't have one. There's a very real tendency to create what you think the answer may be and then offer it as your best guess disguised as a "fact." If you want to qualify an answer with uncertainty, do so. "I cannot recall the exact date of the meeting, but I believe it was sometime in early 2014" is a much better answer than "yes you're right the meeting did take place on January 5th."

Don't allow yourself to get boxed in – boxing in involves asking a question in such a way that it will be difficult for the witness to testify differently later in the deposition, or at trial. I have been boxed in numerous times before, and it can happen very easily if the witness is not on guard against this tactic. One clear signal is questions that begin with the phrase "would you agree that… "followed by an alleged statement of fact concerning a key element in the case. I am asked routinely in security litigation cases to agree with the statement that "when performed competently and professionally security officer services will deter and prevent criminal activity." Sounds harmless enough, but a quick and reassuring "oh yes of course" response from the witness can lead into several damning follow-up questions. My somewhat standard response to that garden-variety question is typically "security officer services are designed to deter certain activity, but prevention is something that is extremely difficult to quantify, and the presence of a security officer, or even a law enforcement officer for that matter, would not be seen by any reasonable person as an absolute guarantee that no criminal activity will occur."

Don't argue – I must admit this is the one that I personally struggle with when giving depositions. What makes this particularly difficult to overcome, is the fact that occasionally you are dealing with someone who prefers to conduct depositions in an argumentative manner. I am not one who likes to paint with a broad brush when it comes to attorneys, and I have been fortunate to be deposed by some of the most respectful and courteous professionals in the legal world, but I certainly have had my experience with what I refer to as "blowhards." These attorneys feel that intimidation is the most effective tactic when questioning a witness. While giving depositions, I have been accused of withholding evidence, making false statements under oath, and been subjected to the implication that I had no sympathy for the victim.

As I have matured, I have learned that this is much more an issue of strategy, than it is one of personal attacks. I was deposed in a recent indemnification (insurance) case by an attorney who is a family friend that goes back many years. Prior to the session, we reminisced and laughed while swapping mutual stories of prior cases. But as soon as we went on the record, I witnessed an abrupt transformation from a congenial colleague to mortal enemy in a matter of seconds. The only answer that I gave that day that did not prompt an argument was when I spelled my name for the record. Several years ago, I was more than happy to engage in legal fisticuffs, but I have since learned that it is much more effective to calmly and confidently state your position, and while holding firm, allowing the other person to be the one who gets rattled. "You mean to tell me that you run around signing contracts and when it comes time to honor your obligations you think you can just pick and choose which parts apply?" My response: "No sir, we take our obligations under every contract very seriously, but in the present case there is no legal obligation that needs to be honored." Did that calm him down? Of course not! But he eventually gave up and moved on to something else. I have found nothing can neutralize an opposing party's attorney quite like the refusal to play into any attempts to get you upset or make you argumentative. Remain confident, purposeful, and calm.

ELECTRONIC DISCOVERY

Electronic Discovery (e-Discovery) is an area that is taking many companies by surprise since they are not prepared to deal with the implications. So, what is e-discovery? e-Discovery is the electronic aspect of identifying, collecting, and producing electronically stored information (ESI) in response to a request for production in a lawsuit or investigation. ESI includes, but is not limited to, emails, documents, presentations, databases, voicemail, audio and video files, social media, and websites.

The processes and technologies around e-discovery are often complex because of the sheer volume of electronic data produced and stored. Additionally, unlike hardcopy evidence, electronic documents are more dynamic and often contain metadata such as time – date stamps, author and recipient information, and file properties. Preserving the original content and metadata for ESI is required in order to eliminate claims of spoliation or tampering with evidence later in the litigation.

After data is identified by the parties on both sides of a matter, potentially relevant documents (including both electronic and hard-copy materials) are placed under a legal hold – meaning they cannot be modified, deleted, erased, or otherwise destroyed. Potentially relevant data is collected and then extracted, indexed, and placed into a database. At this point, data is analyzed to cull or segregate the clearly nonrelevant documents and emails.

Potentially, security companies can store data in a variety of different cyber environments. This could include customer networks, payroll software and vendor servers, and even employee-owned smart phones and social media sites. This is an evolving area of discovery and one that will get more complex in the coming years. Do not overlook this area when being served request to produce documents. Consult with your attorneys and information technology specialist to make sure that you're recovering and preserving all relevant data.

Social media

Social media has dramatically changed how humans interact with each other and the digital footprint left by individuals on sites such as Facebook, Twitter, LinkedIn, and YouTube must not be discounted when dealing with discovery in a security-related case. Rather, attorneys must embrace social media as a part of the "new normal." Discovery through the lens of social media should not be viewed as new and unfamiliar territory. Posts on social media are just additional ways for individuals to document their lives like diaries, letters, photo albums, or emails. An individual's posts may document things that are seemingly innocuous at the time but could literally make or break a case later. Consider how valuable a time-stamped post on Facebook, documenting an individual's mood or physical state may be to either bolstering or undermining that individual's claim for damages. Attorneys would be remiss to not at least probe to see whether an individual's social media site contains discoverable material or confirm that broad discovery requests – like those seeking all communications about the individual's claims – include communications via social media. While this area is relatively new, it is one that will continue to be a hot topic in the area of discovery.

I recently observed a deposition taken of a plaintiff who was claiming, among other things, that a workplace event had caused her great emotional and physical pain and suffering. She testified that the lingering impact of the incident had caused her to be a virtual "prisoner in her own house" and she rarely, if ever, ventured outside. This may have gone unchallenged, except for the fact that her social media footprint told a vastly different tale.

On her social media pages were dozens of pictures of her on recent vacations, at concerts, and appearing to have a great time and enjoying herself in a variety of different social settings. I am neither a medical doctor nor a psychologist, but in my unqualified opinion she did not resemble any type of "prisoner" I had ever seen. The case is still pending so it is unknown whether or not these images will be ultimately admissible at trial, but they did serve to make the deposition very interesting. But the law will continue addressing the need to utilize social media in civil cases, as a recent Florida case points out.

In 2015, a Florida state appellate court required a plaintiff in a slip-and-fall lawsuit to provide the defendant with photos that she had posted on Facebook, reasoning that individuals have little or no privacy rights to information that they have posted on social media.[5] The plaintiff in this action sued a large department store alleging that she slipped and fell while shopping. During discovery, the defendant requested access to the photos that she posted on Facebook. The state trial court granted their request, but the plaintiff hoping to block any access to her Facebook page, appealed the decision.

In its opinion, the appeals court sided with the department store. The court reasoned that photographs can be seen as one of the facts that are necessary to decide personal injury cases. The court reasoned that testimony alone is insufficient for the court "to grasp what a plaintiff's life was like prior to an accident." The court also found that "If a photograph is worth a thousand words, there is no better portrayal of what an individual's life was like than those photographs the individual has chosen to share through social media before the occurrence of an accident causing injury." The judge went on to state that photographs posted on social media are neither privileged nor protected by a right of privacy, regardless of the user's privacy settings and because the information that an individual shares through social networking websites like Facebook may be copied and disseminated by another, the expectation that such information is private, in the traditional sense of the word, is not a reasonable one.

---

[5]*Nucci v. Target Corp.*, et al., No. 4D14-138 (Fla. 4th DCA Jan. 7, 2015).

So what could this mean for a company-owned or employee-controlled social media site. In summary, they could also be fertile ground for discovery requests from the plaintiff in a negligent security action. Are employees posting about issues at customer sites that could put you in a comprising situation during a negligence action?[6] Are your company controlled social media sites pushing out info that could be valuable in the hands of a plaintiff's attorney?

DISCOVERY IN THE WORLD OF CUSTOMER RELATIONSHIPS

One of my goals in writing this book was to bring the unique perspective of the contractor/customer relationship into the world of litigation. It so often gets lost in the world of legal strategy and the desire to make sure that your interest are protected above all else. You can fully expect that when litigation comes, you will likely have your current customer as a codefendant. When this occurs, throughout different stages of the litigation process interactions with the customer can be problematic and concerning. The discovery phase is one such stage.

As we have already seen, volumes of documents, emails, contracts, and various forms of correspondence will be flying around in the litigation universe. In the course of attempting to defend your company, some interesting questions can arise. Am I being an advocate for my customer? Should I be? Should I make the customer aware of what our side is doing throughout each step of the process? If the answer is yes, how do I do so in a way that protects my company's interest and does not agitate or frustrate our outside counsel or insurance company? Every situation can present different and unique circumstances, but there are several key general factors that can be followed during this stage.

Relationships

It is often said that relationships are never really tested until adversity comes. That is certainly true in the customer service world as well. If you don't have a strong relationship with your customer prior to litigation, you will likely not begin to develop one when you're both on the wrong end of a lawsuit. So this is one more reason to make sure that you have a close

---

[6]The National Labor Relations Board has sought to restrict an employer's ability to control what an employee can or cannot publish on their social media sites. Seek legal counsel prior to enacting any policy aimed at social media behavior. For more information see: NLRB Report on Social Media https://www.scribd.com/doc/95479772/NLRB-on-social-media

and free-flowing relationship with all of your customers. This is particularly important with those customers who are prone to incidents on their property that may give rise to litigation. This will give you the ability later to speak frankly with a customer representative about the situation you find yourselves in. In some situations, it can also allow you the luxury of giving gentle advice to customers who may be inviting future problems. One such incident that comes to mind involves an employment law issue that landed our company and customer in the crosshairs of a legal action.

One of the employees assigned to a large industrial complex had become very close to the customer contact and began to see him as his *de facto* supervisor. This is not uncommon, and frankly, should be expected due to the close proximity of our employees and the employees of our customer. However, there is always a legal danger lurking in the background known as joint employment.[7] In this situation one of our employees became concerned about the treatment he was receiving at the hands of other officers assigned to the same property, that he deemed to be discriminatory. His grievance was against another one of our employees, but rather than availing himself of our open door policy and reporting his concerns to a member of our management team, he chose instead to report it to the customer representative. At this point, the customer representative had already become the "go to" person for all issues at the site, so he did not see anything inherently wrong or unusual when he received a call from the security officer complaining of unfair treatment.

In hindsight, the proper response would have been to gently instruct the employee to contact his true employer and voice his concerns to us, but the customer representative chose instead to take a detailed statement and assure the employee that the matter would be handled. Rather than notifying our company at this critical stage, the customer representative instead launched his own investigation and began questioning our employees. At the conclusion of the investigation, the customer representative did not feel that there was any merit to the complaint, and in an effort to maintain harmony in the workplace, decided to move the complaining officer to a different shift and different post. His rationale was that if the parties were separated there was not any danger of conflict. You probably know how the story ends. The officer who had taken his concerns to the customer representative became

---

[7]Also known as coemployment. If joint employment can be established, a contract employee, such as a security officer, can seek legal redress against the customer for claims such as wrongful termination, and in some cases can even be entitled to benefits only offered to direct employees of the customer. Joint employment can be proven by showing factors just as the customer exercising supervision and control over the contractor employees, directing their efforts, getting directly involved in the hiring and firing, etc.

even more disgruntled and decided to file an administrative action, not only against our company, but against the customer entity as well. The first notice that we received that there was even a problem at the worksite was when we received the notice of his charge U.S. Equal Employment Opportunity Commission (EEOC).

Being sensitive to the fact that customers chose to hire contractors to perform the necessary security functions for a variety of reasons, one of them being to avoid directly employing a number of additional personnel, I wanted to quickly get in front of this issue and try to find a way where they could extract themselves from the situation, since legally it should not be their concern. But as I learned more of the facts, I became thoroughly convinced that the bed they were laying in was one that they themselves had made. And while I still had as my goal to remove this burden off of them, our previous relationship and service to them allowed me to have a rather frank conversation with one of the higher-level customer contacts about the unfortunate missteps. This allowed us the opportunity to not only provide security services, but also to utilize our relationship to further educate them on the dangers of intervening in personnel matters.

I have found many times over the years that providing consistent competent service and building a relationship will serve you very well once it's time to be in the trenches together. If there is mutual trust, the maneuverings of lawyers and insurance companies will not be seen as any attempt to throw each other under the proverbial bus when the going gets tough. I have a habit that when I receive a lawsuit that involves the customer, I will make an initial phone call to the most appropriate customer contact and express our appreciation for their business, and also express our willingness to take whatever steps are necessary to preserve our customer relationship throughout the process of litigation. I do not promise, nor do I guarantee, that we will always be able to do so when it comes to compromising our own interest, or that there may not be a time where we have to speak the truth even if it places them at a disadvantage, but the clear message needs to be sent that this is not our goal.

One of the most uncomfortable deposition situations I can recall from recent memory was when I was forced to testify within a few feet of a corporate security manager who had been a long time customer. We were, of course, codefendants in a case alleging negligent security, and based on the discovery to that point it was quite apparent to me that one of the central themes of the case would be security assessments and recommendations provided by our company to theirs. I also knew that in my deposition I would be asked at some point to explain what process we had employed when recommending certain measures prior to beginning our relationship. I also knew that I would be asked to explain our customer's response to those recommendations. Unlike prime time TV dramas, I did not have the option to plead the fifth. To complicate matters further, the corporate security manager's recollection of whether or not we had offered recommendations was slightly different than mine. Of course they were seeking to prove that they had taken all reasonable steps necessary to secure the premises, and by the way, I felt that they had. But there were some measures that they had chosen not to move forward with.

Knowing that the day was approaching, I advised our outside counsel that I had planned to reach out to this customer contact and explain to him what I envisioned happening during my deposition so that there would be no surprises. I cannot say that our attorney was in wholehearted agreement with my plans, but after assuring him that I would in no way compromise our case, I placed a phone call. The deposition was uncomfortable, especially when I was repeatedly asked to identify that same corporate security manager as the person I had communicated with when the recommendations were submitted, but the prior discussion did serve to immunize us both from serious embarrassment. I was further able to get in testimony that I did not believe that the failure to implement these measures made the property any less safe or that their absence led to the plaintiff's harm. Some companies would consider that to be unnecessary, as it does not seem to be relevant to our defense, and some would argue that we would be better served by passing the buck. But that's not what relationships are based on, and it's certainly not a foundation for long-lasting business partnership.

COMMUNICATION

There is a classic line in the iconic movie *The Godfather* when Marlon Brando's character, Vito Corleone utters the phrase "I'm going to make him an offer he can't refuse" in response to how he was going to secure a favor from someone who needed some extra motivation. There have been many times where I have heard a variation on that theme from well-meaning customers who were seeking to influence our position in a particular case. It is not uncommon to feel as if you have an obligation to take care of your customer in a legal sense because they are the lifeblood of your business.

Maintaining proper communication during pending litigation can sometimes be difficult and delicate. Neither side wants to cross any perceived ethical line in terms of discussing the matter, but at the same time they are in a business relationship that requires that communication continues. And often having honest conversations about the elephant in the room can put both sides at ease. Some of the most productive conversations I've been a part of occurred when the matter was directly addressed, with some ground rules being set. Rarely is the issue personal, if it was, they would not be in business with one another, so the need for honest and open communication is critical to make sure that it does not reach that point. While it is not productive to litigate every fact and circumstance in the case when having routine customer discussions, it is advisable to keep each other informed as to what is going on in their respective camps. Again, this is one area where the attorney and the business person often take divergent paths.

I have been told by several well-meaning attorneys and insurance representatives to "not return that phone call" or "don't provide any information at this time." But the simple fact is that failing to respond to a customer, even one you are involved in litigation with, tends to not have a very positive impact on the overall business mission and goals. While I am always extremely careful about what I say, and certainly what I promise, communication should never be shut down totally just because you're both on the defendant's side of the legal table. Trust is a virtue that is quickly fading in our culture and our business world, but with open communication it is one that will hopefully not erode over the life of a legal action.

Many security professionals are fortunate to spend their entire career without seeing the inside of the courtroom. This does not mean that they necessarily escape any legal actions, but most cases that are filed never make it to trial. But that certainly does not mean that it can't or won't happen. And being ready for the day that it does come can once again be the difference between success and failure.

Chapter 6

Trial survival

It is at once strangely comforting, and somewhat disheartening, that I have only experienced a handful of cases that survived all the way from the initial filing of the complaint to a final jury verdict. On a recent trip to my local courthouse, I ran into an attorney friend whom I have known for many years. I was there to testify in a case where our company was not a party. Upon greeting me, he exclaimed, "you must be lost, this isn't a boardroom it's a court room!" He knew what I have known for some time, people in my position don't spend endless days and nights huddled around defense tables waiting for a judge to issue a ruling, or a jury to decide our fate. In fact, I have often remarked that if I find myself sitting in a courtroom something has usually gone horribly wrong. But ironically, the one thing that I enjoy the most is courtroom work. Growing up, my father was a local district attorney for many years, and I enjoyed nothing more than being around the atmosphere of a trial. Striking a jury, cross-examining witnesses, and making impassioned pleas to the judge was my idea of the perfect profession. This is one of the main reasons that I ultimately decided to obtain my law degree and become a licensed attorney.

I have had the pleasure of representing private parties outside of my role as an in-house counsel for a security company. It is exhilarating, and I find that I'm in my element questioning witnesses or attempting to sway a judge to my way of thinking. Understanding the nuances of juries, and how to find the best way of bringing them to your side of the case, is truly an art and a science. And while hours and hours of preparation and study precede the big show of the trial, for someone who has law in their blood, there is nothing like it.

But the feeling can be vastly different when you're sitting at the defense table literally fighting for your company's short-term legal successes, and in some cases, long-term financial solvency. Fortunately, I have never found myself in a situation where the prospect of losing the case would mean the destruction of the company I serve, but I know many who have been in that exact spot. In that setting, there is no thrill or excitement about the upcoming courtroom drama-only anxiety, worry, and fear about what lies ahead.

A trial can seem to be an endless maze of conferences, motions, and arguments about what appear to be trivial matters. But as I have learned, there can be light at the end of the tunnel.

Prior to jumping into an examination of what to expect at trial, let's look at some alternatives that will often stop you just short of the courthouse door.

SETTLEMENT CONFERENCES[1]

There was another secret that no one told me in law school: most judges don't really enjoy trying cases. Some, if they had their way, would be content to preside over a series of settlement conferences and continually play the role of warning the parties that a trial is an apocalyptic event that should be avoided at all costs. I have witnessed this attitude from many judges on many occasions, but the intent is not always one of simply being adverse to the trial process. Quite often it is necessary for judicial efficiency. If you walk into any courthouse in any city in America you will likely find a docket overrun with cases with no end in sight-with new ones being filed each day. And each plaintiff and defendant believes that their case is the most important one and should be given the highest priority. There are simply not enough days on the calendar to get to them all. For that primary reason, parties are encouraged to explore other ways to resolve their disputes.

In addition to a legal system that is busting at the seams, the wheels of justice turn very slowly. Watch any courtroom-based television drama in primetime and you will see justice being served in less than an hour from opening credits to the verdict. In the real world, the process takes years. I am currently involved in a lawsuit that remains pending even as we recently passed the 8-year anniversary of the incident that gave rise to the litigation. In the months after the filing, some 7 years ago, several attempts were made to settle, but the efforts failed due to strong objections on both sides. I can say with the utmost certainty that many of the parties wish they still had the chance to get out when they still could.

In many jurisdictions, a settlement conference will be required before any case can go to trial. The settlement conference is shorter and much less expensive to conduct than a trial. Accordingly, it can be attractive to all involved to reach a settlement. A judge typically presides at the conference in their chambers or a private conference room. The requirements for attending a settlement conference may vary by jurisdiction. However, both parties

---

[1]Another alternative dispute method is a process known as Arbitration. Its use is rare in the context of security litigation due to the fact that most actions are brought by third parties who are not privy to any agreement not to file lawsuit in court.

with their legal counsel are usually required to attend. In most cases, any parties or individuals who have the authority to potentially settle the matter are required to attend.

The proceedings of a settlement conference can vary widely between jurisdictions and even between judges. Typically, both sides must inform the judge about the case in advance. This may include disclosing certain facts and evidence that supports that party's side of the case. This way, the judge is reasonably well apprised of the case before the conference occurs. Should a settlement agreement be reached, the judge asks the attorneys to prepare a memorandum that specifies the terms of the settlement. This formal settlement agreement is signed by all the parties. After it is signed and filed, the judge formally dismisses the lawsuit.

MEDIATION

Traditional litigation is a mistake that must be corrected... For some disputes trials will be the only means, but for many claims trials by adversarial contest must in time go the way of the ancient trial by battle and blood. Our system is too costly, too painful, too destructive, and too inefficient for really civilized people.
Chief Justice Warren E. Burger, (Ret.) US Supreme Court

When former Chief Justice Burger made that statement at a 1984 meeting of the American Bar Association, he was attempting to make the point that the resolution of a dispute, rather than "winning" in a court of law, should be the ultimate aim of the parties. It is true that some cases can only be truly resolved by having a judge or jury decide it based on the merits, but for many others alternatives are necessary.

Mediation is a formal dispute resolution process that usually presents you with the best chance to settle a lawsuit that has been filed against the security company before trial. As a general rule, you will likely experience a mediation session at some point in the life of the case, if the action persists beyond initial attempts to settle. Many defendants are nervous going into mediation – don't be. There is no winner or loser at mediation. And in most cases it is completely voluntary, although many judges will order the parties to explore settlement through this process prior to a trial date being set. No issues affecting your lawsuit, aside from whether it settles, are decided at mediation. You will not have to "perform" at your mediation or answer questions, as you would at a trail or at a deposition. Your sole purpose at the mediation is to have the final word on whether your case settles. It can be a long day, or in some cases multiple days, and I often have wondered what value my presence was, since all I was doing was sitting in a small room with my attorneys waiting for the other side to make a move. But I learned many valuable lessons in mediations about how cases are viewed, and how plaintiffs go about structuring their cases and arguments. At one point in my career, I was somewhat adverse to the process of mediation as I saw it as a forum designed to see who would blink first and cave into the other side's demands, but I now view it as a real opportunity to potentially put the matter behind us – if the parties are willing. A wise mediator once told me that if mediation is successful, "both sides will leave wishing they had gotten more; and neither will feel too much like a winner or loser." It truly is about compromise, not about who comes out on top.

Most lawyers will have a face-to-face meeting with their clients prior to mediation to discuss what mediation entails and to get authority to settle your case for a certain amount (in the vast majority of actions this authority will rest with your insurance company). At a minimum, in negligent security mediation, the people who will attend will be: a representative from your company, your lawyer, the plaintiff's lawyer (and usually the plaintiff), a representative from your insurance company, and the mediator. The point of mediation is to get the people who hold the "final authority" to settle the case together.

A mediator is simply another party, in most cases a lawyer, who has no connection to either party in the lawsuit and no interest in the outcome of the lawsuit. The mediator must be agreed upon by both your attorney and the opposing counsel (if the attorneys can't agree on a mediator, the court will appoint one, which neither side wants). Some lawyers are full-time mediators and no longer represent clients. Some still represent clients and can be either a plaintiffs' or defense attorney. Don't worry if your mediator is also a plaintiff's attorney. He is not the plaintiff attorney on your case, and he would not last long as a mediator if he showed bias toward the other side. Some of the best mediators I have dealt with were also current attorneys. The role of the mediator is primarily to act as a buffer between the two parties during negotiations.

Everything that it said in the mediation is confidential and cannot be used in court. The plaintiff's attorney can't crossexamine you at trial and ask "Didn't you say at mediation … ." However, should you reveal a new witness or document at the mediation, the opposing attorney can certainly find these people afterward and get information from them. A good rule of thumb is that while statements themselves can't be used against you, the information in those statements may. Likewise, the mediator cannot, and will not, testify later in court about anything that is said during the session.

The mediator does not take sides and will not give either side and as a rule, will typically give legal advice about their case. Although, a good mediator can be an excellent sounding board for what to expect if the case should proceed. The mediator's job is not to determine a winner or loser, but merely to facilitate communication between the two sides and help the two sides reach a settlement. He may play devil's advocate while alone with each side in an attempt to help them see the other's point of view. The purpose of mediation is to allow each side to fully explore the risk factors that affect their case. This will usually be the only opportunity that each of the parties' attorneys has, to point out the risks facing the other side directly to the opposing party, with the possible exception of a formal settlement conference. In order for your case to settle, each side will have to compromise. The plaintiff should not expect to get everything that they potentially would get if they won at trial. At mediation, you control the outcome of your case. At trial, the jury will. Jury trials are uncertain affairs under the best of circumstances. If you successfully settle your case at mediation, the mediator will prepare a settlement agreement for all parties to sign. You will likely have to sign a release and in many cases, a confidentiality agreement.

If your mediation results in an impasse (the two sides cannot reach a compromise), your lawsuit will just continue as if the mediation never occurred. However, all hope for settlement is not lost. I have had several cases that ultimately settled after a failed mediation (some within days). Both sides tend to want to revisit settlement possibilities when trial approaches. However, do not take mediation lightly because you expect the case to settle at some time down the road. Mediation is usually your best chance to settle.

I have attended many more mediations than trials. Depending on the parties involved, they can be extremely informal with both sides sitting around the table discussing how to resolve the dispute, but I've also been involved in very elaborate productions with attorneys using PowerPoint presentations, and even in one case attempting to have witnesses testify in order to simulate a mock trial and show us "what we would be facing." If you are dealing with a seasoned and well-qualified mediator, he or she can be extremely effective in bringing the parties together. As the security company representative, if you are involved in the sessions, often you will be sitting there wondering, "why do we not take this offer?" or in some cases, "why did we take this offer?" There can be an overwhelming feeling of powerlessness, especially when it feels you are only present because it is required. After being involved in many sessions, I have come to clearly define my role in these matters.

Being an attorney, I am often asked in mediation sessions, usually by my own legal team, to get involved in the legal aspect of the discussions and negotiations. I'm happy to do so, but also have to focus my efforts and attention on what any proposed settlement means for my company. This can sometimes mean putting the law aside and trying to push forward for a resolution that may be in our best interest economically, or based merely on the fact that a trial seems to be unwise based on the known and unknown factors.

In addition, I believe that the presence of a security company representative in the room can play a valuable role in making sure that the facts are clear and accurate. My personality does not lend itself very well to sitting in a general mediation session where both sides are giving their opening statements, and then hearing the plaintiff's attorney misstate fact after fact about our company or what the security officer did or did not do. I have to stop myself from wanting to jump up and correct these errors and set the record straight. While the setting of an opening session in front of all the attorneys from both sides, and the mediator, is not the proper time for this, I believe it is very important to attend these mediation sessions to serve as a guidepost when there is a question about the facts of the case. The attorneys that you deal with are likely handling large caseloads, and while I'm sure you will be dealing with professional and competent lawyers, often they may not have a comprehensive and thorough grasp of the facts, certainly not to the level that you will possess. There have been multiple occasions in private sessions during the mediation conference that I am able to point out inaccuracies in the plaintiff's case, or assist the mediator in understanding our business from a real-world perspective.

The bottom line is to never dismiss mediation as just a formality on the way to trial. It can be a meaningful process, and in some cases, one that can potentially save you years of time and expense. While this is dependent upon the parties' reasonableness and willingness to settle, you should go into this process with a genuine optimism that it may afford you your last opportunity to put the matter to rest before walking into court.

THE TRIAL

Many perceptions of trials are formed based on media portrayals, and what we assume takes place when lawyers, judges, and parties draw battle lines in order to find justice for a particular situation. The reality sometimes can be much different than fiction. As boring as it sounds, I actually enjoy sitting in courtrooms and observing routine tasks being handled. Even a flooded traffic citation docket is fascinating to me. To watch the process that was laid out in our constitution and subsequently volumes of law, is to observe a system that at its best treats everyone equally and affords the opportunity to seek justice. Is the system perfect? No – far from it. I've come to realize that it never will be perfect. It certainly needs changes to be made, but I also feel that it is the best system on earth.

But even with its merits and lofty ideals, the courtroom can be a very intimidating and lonely place. For the first time participant, being on the witness stand, sitting at the defense table, or even observing, can be a daunting and overwhelming experience. Once again, learning as much as you can before the trial day arrives, can pay enormous dividends when you find yourself in a real situation. I value my legal education and there is no way that I could effectively carry out my duties without it, but if I'm being honest, I must admit that some of the best lessons I actually learned were not found in the classroom, or even on the bar exam, but by observing other attorneys. I once heard an interview with a famous musician who was world renowned as a guitar virtuoso. When he was asked how he first learned to play the instrument, he explained that as a boy he would slow down the speed of his record player to a point where every note could be identifiable. He would then learn the song note by painstaking note until he could play them in succession and at the original tempo. Being an effective attorney, an effective witness, and even an effective party can follow a similar process.

When I have had the opportunity to represent a party in court, I often use the techniques and styles I have seen others utilize. Even the words that I use, the questions that I ask, and the points that I attempt to drive home are in many cases merely an attempt to imitate great litigators whom I have observed in other cases. I have come to realize that the best way to learn the "song" of a trial is to practice it note for note. So the first step in being successful at trial is knowing what to expect and how to handle it. Let's look at the process of the trial, and then we'll see a real-world application of what can happen when the stakes are high.

Of course each case starts off with the filing of a lawsuit by the plaintiff alleging various claims. After discovery, which in most cases can take months if not years, and after the efforts to settle have failed, the next step is to try the case. In a civil trial, a judge or jury examines the evidence to decide whether, by a "preponderance of the evidence,[2]" the defendant should be held legally responsible for the damages alleged by the plaintiff. A trial is the plaintiff's opportunity to argue his or her case, in the hope of obtaining a judgment against the security company. A complete civil trial typically consists of six main phases, each of which is described in more detail later:

---

[2]This is a different standard than "beyond a reasonable doubt" used in criminal cases. A "preponderance of evidence" means that a party has shown that the evidence it presents relating to facts, causes, damages, or fault is more likely than not the correct version.

choosing a jury, opening statements, witness testimony crossexamination, closing arguments, jury instruction, jury deliberation, and the verdict

Choosing a Jury, except in cases that are tried only before a judge, is one of the first steps in any civil trial. During jury selection, the judge (and usually the plaintiff and the defendant through their respective attorneys) will question a pool of potential jurors generally and as to matters pertaining to the particular case – including personal ideological predispositions or life experiences that may pertain to the case. The judge can excuse potential jurors at this stage, based on their responses to questioning. In many high-stakes cases, the services of a jury consultant may be employed in order to select the best panel possible to hear your matter. Also at this stage, both the plaintiff and the defendant may exclude a certain number of jurors through use of "peremptory challenges" and challenges "for cause." A peremptory challenge can be used to exclude a juror for any reason and a challenge for cause can be used to exclude a juror who has shown that he or she cannot be truly objective in deciding the case. Once a jury is selected, the first "dialog" in the trial comes in the form of two opening statements – one from the plaintiff's attorney and the other from an attorney representing the defendant.

No witnesses testify at this stage, and no physical evidence is ordinarily utilized. Because the plaintiff must demonstrate the defendant's legal liability based on the plaintiff's allegations, the plaintiff's opening statement is usually given first, and is often more detailed than that of the defendant. In some cases, the defendant may wait until the conclusion of the plaintiff's main case before making their own opening statement. The plaintiff presents the facts of the case and the defendant's alleged role in causing the plaintiff's damages (or reasons to find for the plaintiff) – basically walking the jury through what the plaintiff intends to demonstrate in order to get a civil judgment against the defendant. The defendant's attorney gives the jury the defense's own interpretation of the facts, and sets the stage for rebutting the plaintiff's key evidence and presenting any "affirmative" defenses to the plaintiff's allegations (or reasons to find for the security company). When a civil lawsuit involves multiple parties (i.e., when your customer or insurance company may also be individual defendants), attorneys representing each party may give their own distinct opening arguments.

At the heart of any civil trial is, what is often called, the "case-in-chief," the stage at which each side presents its key evidence and arguments to the jury. In its case-in-chief, the plaintiff methodically sets forth their evidence in an attempt to convince the jury that the security company is legally responsible for the plaintiff's damages, or that judgment for the plaintiff is warranted under the circumstances. It is at this point that the plaintiff may call witnesses and security experts to testify, in order to strengthen his or her case. The plaintiff may also introduce physical evidence, such as photographs, documents, and other pieces of tangible evidence. Whether a witness is called by the plaintiff or the defendant, the witness testimony process usually adheres to the following formula: the witness is called to the stand and is "sworn in," taking an oath to tell the truth. The party who called the witness to the stand questions the witness through "direct" examination, eliciting information through question-and-answer, to strengthen the party's position in the dispute. After direct examination, the opposing party has an opportunity to question the witness through "crossexamination" – attempting to poke holes in the witness's story, attack their credibility, or otherwise discredit the witness and his or her testimony.

After crossexamination, the side that originally called the witness has a second opportunity to question him or her, through "redirect examination," and attempt to remedy any damaging effects of crossexamination. After the plaintiff concludes its case-in-chief and "rests," the defendant can present its own evidence in the same proactive manner, seeking to show that it is not liable for the plaintiff's claimed harm. The defense may call its own witnesses to the stand, and can present any of its own independent evidence in an effort to refute or downplay the key elements of the plaintiff's legal allegations. At this point, the security company will often offer its own security expert to either refute the plaintiff's expert or establish what they view as "reasonable" security measures.

Similar to the opening statement, the closing argument offers the plaintiff and the defendant, in a civil dispute, a chance to "sum up" the case, recapping the evidence in a light favorable to their respective positions. This is the final chance for the parties to address the jury prior to the deliberations, so in closing arguments the plaintiff seeks to show why the evidence requires the jury to find the defendant legally responsible for the plaintiff's damages, or why the plaintiff's case is stronger than the defendant's. In turn, the defendant tries to show that the plaintiff has fallen short of establishing the defendant's liability for any civil judgment in the plaintiff's favor. After both sides of the case have had a chance to present their evidence and make a closing argument, the next step toward a verdict is the jury instruction – a process in which the judge gives the jury the set of legal standards it will need to decide whether the defendant should be held accountable for the plaintiff's alleged harm. The judge decides what legal standards should apply to the defendant's case, based on the civil claims at issue and the evidence presented during the trial. Often, this process takes place with input and argument from both the plaintiff and the defendant. The judge then instructs the jury on those relevant legal principles decided upon; including the findings that the jury will need to make in order to arrive at certain conclusions. The judge also describes the key concepts, such as the "preponderance of the evidence" legal standard; defines any specific claims that the jury may consider; and discusses different types of damages (i.e. compensatory and punitive) – all based on the evidence presented at trial. The case then goes "to the jury."

After receiving instructions from the judge, the jurors, as a group, consider the case through a process called "deliberation," attempting to agree on whether the defendant should be held liable based on the plaintiff's claims, and if so, the appropriate compensation for any damages. Deliberation is the first opportunity for the jury to discuss the case – a methodical process that can last from a few hours to several days. Once the jury reaches a decision, the jury foreperson informs the judge, and the judge usually announces the verdict in open court. Most states require that a 12-person jury in a personal injury case be unanimous in finding for the plaintiff or the defendant, though some states allow for verdicts based on a majority as low as 9 to 3. If the jury fails to reach a unanimous (or sufficient majority) verdict and finds itself at a standstill (a "hung" jury), the judge may declare a "mistrial," after which the case may be dismissed or the trial may start over again from the jury selection stage.

If you have not had previous courtroom experience, make it a point to visit the court and listen to others testify. This is the best way to understand and familiarize yourself with what you will face as a witness without taking the stand yourself. At trial, an effective courtroom performance is founded upon experience and diligent preparation. Before taking the stand, you should be thoroughly familiar with all the reports prepared by you, and all the statements or depositions given by you. Any change in testimony at trial may result in impeachment by plaintiff's counsel and points scored by his client. You will be asked what you did to prepare for the testimony, and this should not been seen as a threatening question. It is acceptable to state that you reviewed the relevant material. You cannot be asked about the content of discussions you have had with your attorney.

If you are serving as the security company representative at trial, you may be forced to sit through hours, sometimes days, of proceedings. Here are some important tips I have gathered to navigate the process of testifying and interacting in the courtroom.

Always tell the truth. At trial, as in all other matters, honesty is the best policy. If you tell the truth and tell it accurately, nobody can cross you up. Do not guess or make up an answer. If you do not know the answer, it is best to say, "I don't know." If you are asked about details that you do not remember. it is best to say, "I don't remember."

Be attentive. You should remain alert at all times so that you can hear, understand, and give a proper response to each question. If the judge or jury get the impression that you are bored or indifferent, they may tend to disregard your testimony.

Take your time and speak clearly and loudly. Give the question such thought as it requires to understand it. The juror farthest from you should be able to hear distinctly what you have to say. Since all testimony is recorded, do not nod your head "yes" or "no."

Answer all questions directly. Answer only the questions that have been asked, then stop. Avoid "volunteering" information. If you do not understand a question, ask that it be explained. Do not look at the lawyer for help while you are testifying and never ask the Judge if you have to answer. You are on your own. This will give the jury the impression that you are holding something back.

Be serious in the Courtroom. Avoid joking and wisecracks in the jury's presence. This includes hallway actions and conversations.

Do not lose your temper. Remember that some attorneys may attempt to wear you down so that you will lose your temper and say things that are not correct. Hold your temper and your testimony will be much more valuable. Do not fence or argue with the attorneys. They have a right to question you, and many are expert in this craft.

Stay away from traps. If you make an estimate, make sure that everyone understands that you are estimating. Be cautious of questions asking if you are willing to swear to your version of the events. You were "sworn" to tell the truth when you took the stand, do not be afraid of saying so. Beware of questions asking you if another witness was telling the truth or lying. You can only tell the truth based upon your observations. You have no way of knowing what another person observed, especially when you did not hear that person testify.

Give positive, definite answers when at all possible. Avoid saying, "I think, I believe, in my opinion." A witness testifies to facts, not beliefs, or opinions. Do not say, "That's all that happened." Cover yourself, and say, "That's all I recall." Later in your testimony, you may remember more details.

Be yourself. Do not use "legalese" or security "lingo" just for the sake of impressing the jury. It will have the opposite effect.

The most effective witness is the one who can tell their story comfortably. Just tell the truth and be yourself. Everything else will take care of itself.

EXPERT WITNESSES

Normally, courts prohibit witnesses from testifying based on their own opinions or analysis. In fact, it is likely that when you are deposed or testify in court, you can be sure that an objection from the opposing attorney will be close behind if you are asked to speculate based on your own opinion. There is one major exception to this rule, and that involves the use of expert testimony.

Expert testimony is a vital component to proving, or disproving, a negligent security action. Experts are used as a link in the chain, attempting to tie the security company to the incident by lack of taking adequate precautions to prevent it. There are many former law enforcement personnel and veteran security professionals who have made a living out of offering expert testimony on both sides of the civil bar. And to address the obvious and the most often quoted criticism of expert witnesses, they are paid to give their opinions. This is fertile ground to attack the witnesses' credibility before and during trial, but in my experience, the fact that they are a "hired gun" will not automatically dilute or discredit anything that they say.

As a general rule, you can assume that whatever has been alleged by the plaintiff to be lacking in the situation that gave rise to the lawsuit (more officers, gates, lighting, etc.), there is a security expert who is willing to state that its absence is a proof of negligence, and if it had been included the harm would have been prevented. For example, if you are dealing with a case that involves the introduction of a weapon into the workplace, you can be guaranteed that an expert will likely be retained who will state emphatically that a metal detector should have been placed at that access point and all the employees and visitors should have been checked for weapons prior to entering. This is the expert telling the jury that in essence, the company failed to meet a professional standard. I have faced this a number of times, and the difficulty with such testimony is that it is given with the benefit of complete hindsight. Nevertheless, expert testimony can be very powerful and effective in leading juries down the path to the plaintiff's way of thinking.

Conversely, an effective expert witness can be a great asset for the security company's defenses as well. While the defense expert may have a tougher time, he or she can provide valuable information in testimony as to what truly should be deemed reasonable and what should not. It is always somewhat frustrating when security measures are deemed to be standard after an event, when they may not have been deemed to be so before something bad happened. I can recall one experience with a security expert, who was retained by the plaintiff in a premises liability case. The underlying event was an attack, with a weapon, that occurred in the workplace. There was no real foreseeability and the attack was totally unexpected, even from the plaintiff's point of view. But nevertheless, the hired expert was willing to state emphatically that each workplace should have a policy of "patting down" or searching the belongings of every employee who reported for work. While it was debatable whether or not this would have even prevented the attack, I certainly did not see it as being reasonable or realistic within the context of that particular set of facts. Allow me to quickly prove that point. I am supremely confident that less than 50% of the people reading this book were subjected to being searched or checked for weapons when you reported for work this morning. Furthermore, it is highly unlikely that you encountered any such process while visiting other companies or places of business, unless it was in a high-risk environment such as an airport, courthouse, or other environment where criminal activity is likely or expected. But if something were to occur in those environments that currently allow access without a mandatory search for weapons, there would be no shortage of experts to claim that it was unreasonable not to have those measures in place.

Blaming the victim

In many ways, a trial is like a theatrical production. There is staging, props, and each participant is expected to play a role. Even such seemingly inconsequential factors as how parties react to certain events in the courtroom may be scrutinized by the judges and juries alike. If you find yourself as a first time participant in a trial, simple tasks such as what to do during breaks may appear to be orchestrated and guided by your attorney whose purpose is to make sure that you are putting on the most effective case possible from the opening arguments to the verdict. The first time I attended a trial as a corporate defendant, there were discussions about what kind of car I planned to drive to the courthouse, my attire, and how I should act when the plaintiff was testifying. One area that needs to be considered is how the victim is perceived and ultimately treated during the proceedings.

Before your mind is flooded with incorrect assumptions, or confusion as to why this topic is being broached, let me state a couple of things very clearly. First and foremost, it is usually not a good legal strategy to place the sole blame on the victim for his or her injury or loss. While this may be appropriate if you're dealing with a party who suffered the loss of product, equipment, or property due to the fact that they failed to accept the recommendations for security measures, or did not expend enough resources to prevent the occurrence, it should be used with the utmost caution when dealing with someone who has suffered a life-altering event. We're also not talking about someone who ignored numerous "wet floor" signs before proceeding past them and ultimately suffering an injury. I have been involved in those cases as well, and your main legal strategy may be very well to put the blame on the "victim." But when dealing with someone whose life has been changed forever by a criminal action, occurring at one of your customer locations, you're not going to get very far by pointing the finger at the victim and indicating that they bear some responsibility.[3]

You are probably thinking that this is not a tactic that normally would spring to mind when preparing to defend a lawsuit, so why address it? Because it does come up, in various ways, in many trials. Sometimes, in very inarticulate ways.

I had a rather unique experience that brought this matter front and center several years ago. In one of the most bizarre and illogical cases I have ever encountered, I was faced with a plaintiff who I was not entirely sure at the time was a true victim. It has since become known as the "person who sued themselves" case when I relate the story to friends and colleagues. Late one evening, I received a phone call from one of our local management representatives informing me that there had been an apparent attack on a security officer who was on duty. The physical injuries appeared to be minor, but the incident was very serious due to the nature of what the security officer was alleging. The officer on duty had been patrolling in an area outside of an industrial manufacturing plant when she alleged that someone had emerged from the shadows and assaulted her.

I began the normal process of Workmen's Compensation filings and attempted to reach out to the officer to see if she was okay and to offer the services of the company to assist her through this ordeal. Within 24 hours of the incident, the officer had retained counsel and refused to speak to anyone at our company or participate in the investigative process. This certainly raised some red flags in my mind, but she was certainly entitled to retain counsel to represent her interests if she felt doing so was appropriate. Local law enforcement handled the criminal investigation and sought to find the alleged assailant. Shortly thereafter, the lawsuit arrived.

We, along with our customer, were subsequently sued by the officer alleging, among other things, that there was inadequate security at the property and this fact contributed to her injury. Let that sink in for a minute. We were now facing a lawsuit filed by a security officer, alleging inadequate security, for an injury that happened at a site – where she was the security

---

[3]Many states do allow some fault to be apportioned to the "victim" and the perpetrator in liability cases. This is a decision for the jury to make and can impact the amount of damages that are ultimately recovered by the plaintiff. Depending on the case, this may be something an attorney argues in order to reduce and award.

officer. There were other allegations made by the security officer, among other things that she was not trained properly, and based on her obvious lack of qualifications, never should have been hired. Another claim that at the time that I had yet to encounter in my career was "you should have known better than to hire me." I felt that the case could have easily been defended on the training and hiring counts because the officer received all of the state required training, as well as internal company instruction, but the issue of what responsibility she bore in the matter was a little more delicate.

Let me emphasize that I did not know then, nor do I know today, that the assault in fact did not happen. I was not there, and I have no reason to believe that the officer was being anything but truthful when she made the report to the police, or in her legal complaint. But the whole situation at that time seemed odd to me and I could not shake the feeling of wondering what had actually occurred? As my deposition date drew near, I was continually bothered by some of the facts and I felt that when the questions came about the assault, I must address my suspicions.

As we were nearing the heart of my deposition, the questions eventually tuned to the incident that had brought us all to that point. The room was full of our attorneys, the plaintiff's team, and even our customer's legal representatives. Then the first question came asking me some details about what could have been done differently to avoid the assault on the plaintiff. Thinking that I needed to somehow "be on the record" about my doubts, I began my answer with "Assuming that the assault happened …" Depositions can be exciting events and there can be some energetic moments, but for the most part they consist of a group of people passively listening and occasionally even losing interest in what is going on, but when I uttered those words, every head in the room shot up. My attorney, my customer, and I am pretty sure even the court reporter, looked at me, as if to say "Why would you go there?" Of course the plaintiff's attorney, who was a very well-respected and effective litigator, seized on my attempt to be semiaccusatory and challenged me to back up my statement with facts to show that there was any reason to believe that anything other than what the plaintiff had alleged had actually occurred. After a lame attempt to explain that "the police were still investigating the matter so it had not been determined what actually happened," I realized that my attempt to inject doubt about the central theme of the case had done much more harm than good.

I learned a valuable lesson that day. Leave it to the attorneys to make any legal arguments that may be needed to "attack" the vulnerabilities concerning the plaintiff's version of events. I have been asked many times during depositions if I believe that the plaintiff is telling the truth, or if the event happened. Unless I have hard evidence to the contrary, I don't pretend to know either way. My standard response is "I was not there and all I can speak to is what the investigation has revealed." When you make it into court, the juries will in most cases already be sympathetic to the victim's case, and you must always be aware that you can cause them to identify with them even more if you come across as uncaring or unfeeling. Let the lawyer handle that. A company must be very cautious before engaging in a trial strategy that includes blaming the victim, as this tactical approach could backfire, resulting in a higher verdict in response.

Profits versus people

I have often said that a trial will put a business at a disadvantage right out of the gate. When it comes to comparing a victim who has suffered an injury against a corporation, or other business entity, there is no debating which side will ultimately be seen as a more sympathetic figure. Juries can relate to victims and real people. They see themselves in the face of those who have been harmed and are now seeking justice. But it is much more difficult for a company to appear "human" in the courtroom. Add to this, the natural tendency to hold security companies responsible when things go wrong, and it is easy to see the beginnings of a perfect storm. If a criminal act happens, then it must mean that the security was not very effective, right? If I were not in this business, that is an assumption that I would likely make. Often the average citizen is not going to dig deeper into the intricacies of liability and what really is the driving force behind some incidents. I have overheard many conversations that paint a picture of a security force as unflattering just because a workplace shooter successfully entered a business and committed a horrific act. These are, of course, serious situations, and ones that cry out for tough questions to be asked and answered, but it does not automatically mean that negligence was involved. In addition to this rush to judgment, businesses are often demonized for an alleged pursuit of profit at the expense of people.

A security company should never be made to feel that they have to be apologetic for turning a profit, or in some situations, merely seeking to turn a profit. Likewise, our customers are in the situation of attempting to do the same thing. This means that budgets are not unlimited and the amount of resources that a company can expand on security services is but one line item in the larger organizational context. But the dollars spent on security, or often a lack thereof, can come under tremendous scrutiny when dealing with the aftermath of a security breach or a criminal attack. I'm sure that any security professional would agree that it would be much easier to provide our services with no financial restraints and virtually unlimited resources targeted toward security measures at the site level, but we must play the hand were dealt, and this often means doing more with less.

This can make tasks such as conducting a thorough risk assessment, and more importantly, implementing measures, difficult to fully achieve. We still live in the era of having to watch every penny and being as efficient as we possibly can, while at the same time, providing a high level of security that protects the customers, employees, and visitors. This can be a delicate balancing act, but one more security companies are growing accustomed to and are able to deal with effectively. But in the realm of litigation, this topic can rear its head time and time again and will cause the customer and security company alike to use great caution in how they respond to it.

One of the reasons the argument of "people vs. profits" in security-related lawsuits are so strong for the plaintiff is the simple fact that quite often the answer as to why there were not more security measures in place is, in fact, resource-based. Admittedly, lack of funds is the reason that many things are not accomplished or implemented, not just security measures. But in the area of keeping people safe, the average person would surmise that no amount is too great to spend to stop something bad from happening. To use the same logic, any police force in every big city or small town in America should be quadrupled overnight because money is no object. However, this would of course result in increased taxes and fees, and would surely elicit a strong protest from the taxpayer. The same is true of business. Everyone has to be price conscious, so unlimited budgets in any realm are not feasible or realistic.

Many times, I have been backed into a corner in depositions with questions as to why additional measures were not put in place. "Why only have two officers, why not six or eight or ten?" The answer is pretty simple: who is going to pay for it? I've even heard one expert in a security case give testimony that even if the customer did not agree to fund additional measures, it was incumbent upon the security company to fund the measures themselves. Obviously this person did not have a fundamental understanding of how our business works or how the pricing models are arrived at. But nevertheless, this tactic can be very effective in the eyes of the jury.

Think for a minute; is there any price too high to ensure the safety of your loved ones? Of course not. And I would say the same, and plaintiff attorneys know our sensibilities in these areas. So you must plan to effectively respond to this issue. When in a deposition, or when giving testimony in court, I have a general rule never to answer a question by citing a lack of funding. And by the way, a lack of funding is usually not the main reason that measures are not implemented. It comes back to reasonableness. "Could there have been five security officers on the property? Sure, but that would not have been reasonable." That is an adequate and correct answer, and is much better than "yes I would have loved to have had five officers, but who is going to pay for it?"

This theme will be hammered home in many security cases that you deal with. I recently read a case, where during the discovery phase, the plaintiff was able to acquire internal financial reports from a residential property management firm. The reports reflected that the landscaping budget at a particular property where a homicide had occurred, was almost twice the amount on a yearly basis than that which was being spent on security services. That is powerful information to put before a jury to show that an entity was more concerned about profit than the safety of its people. We may know that this is not always the case, but you have to be prepared to address it effectively in order to diminish the impact this type of information will have at trial.

Now that we've seen how a trial typically operates, let's put that knowledge into practice. There are many cases reported each year that deal with security liability and the dynamic of the customer and security company relationships, but let's look at one from recent years that has many of the different elements that you can expect to face when you are forced to sit in the defendant's chair.

Several years ago, a nationally recognized security company was asked to provide services to a large hospital campus in Florida. The hospital also employed in-house security officers and off-duty police officers as a part of its security program. Two officers were assigned to the property and their primary duties were restricted to the parking and exterior areas of the campus. They were asked to serve as a deterrent by executing patrols and reporting any unusual or criminal activity. The security company had begun service in the year 2000 and its role had incrementally been diminished by the hospital over the years until it was limited to the exterior presence. In response to a tragedy that happened in 2006, the company would find themselves as a defendant in a negligent security lawsuit and forced to defend itself against claims that it should have done more.[4]

On November 20, 2006, at approximately 9:00 am, a 37-year-old pregnant wife and mother of two, who had been working in the hospital's pharmacy as a supervisor since 2002, was on duty when a disgruntled patient entered the facility. The supervisor was familiar with the patient, as she had encountered

---

[4]Derrick McCants v. Wackenhut Corporation, Case Number: 16-2008-CV-014834 Circuit Court, Duval County, Florida.

her before. Three days prior to this day, the supervisor had chided the patient for attempting to jump further ahead in line in front of others who were waiting to be seen. On this day, the patient once again became disruptive and was seen arguing with another pharmacy employee. Hoping to diffuse the situation, the supervisor approached the disturbed patient and attempted to calm her down. At some point, the patient pulled a gun from her purse and shot the pharmacy supervisor five times killing her. In July, prior to this shooting in November, there was another incident involving the disturbed patient at the same hospital. During that encounter a 53-year-old woman told the police that a stranger had approached her on the hospital's fourth floor and said "you know me" before brandishing a knife. It was later determined that the suspect in that incident was the same woman who later killed the pharmacy employee. It was also reported that the shooter had slapped another nurse in the face on at least one prior occasion, before that fateful day in the pharmacy. The murder of an innocent employee is no doubt an unspeakable tragedy that naturally leaves the family of the victim asking why and how something like this could happen? As with many of these types of workplace crimes, they turned to the civil justice system to find the answers.

The estate of the young victim brought a lawsuit against the security company claiming that they were negligent in providing its services to the hospital, and because of this failure, the victim was killed.[5] They argued that the security company should have been much more proactive in taking on the responsibility of advising the hospital on what security measures should have been taken to prevent occurrences, such as the one that took the victim's life. The central theme of the case would be who the decider really was.

But before we dig deeper into the facts, let's consider a few realities about this particular situation. The setting for this horrible event was a hospital. An environment, that while is certainly in need of adequate security, cannot function properly without some sense of openness and reasonable access to the individuals in need of its services. This was not a case of a nefarious character breaching layers of security and carrying out a diabolical plan, it was an act of senseless violence carried out by an obviously disturbed and deranged person who saw no other way to handle her problems except by committing a heinous crime. The criminal justice system handled her punishment by sending her to prison for life, but that is rarely enough to satisfy the desire for understanding and justice for the family that remains to mourn a lost loved one.

---

[5]It is unclear if the family of the victim has ever filed a lawsuit against the hospital or if a settlement was ever reached between the two parties, as court records show no history.

The central and overriding theme against the security company in this case was who the ultimate decision maker was in regard to what security measure would be implemented, and prior to that, what measures should have been suggested by the security company. The case heavily focused on the security company's role at the hospital, as well as a series of annual security surveys that the company performed at the facility. As part of their services, the security company conducted limited assessments with the goal of evaluating certain aspects of its services and the security program at the hospital. None of the surveys done before the shooting, including the one dated just 3 months prior, ever mentioned the pharmacy or included any recommendations to the hospital as a whole.

If you find yourself in the defendant's chair in a similar action, you can fully expect that your process of evaluating your customer's property and current procedures will be heavily scrutinized and you will be forced to explain your methodology and ultimate conclusions. In this case, the local security company manager explained that the surveys were more of a "marketing tool" and only included the areas to which they were assigned. Although, they played a much more prominent role in the overall security program in previous years, by the time of the shooting, the company's officers were used at only two locations, both in parking lots far away from the pharmacy where the shooting took place. So what could the company have been reasonably expected to do in regard to preventing violence in the pharmacy area? Surprisingly, the security company seemed to have an ally in the hospital representative who did not appear to have expected the contractor to guide the decisions about internal policies and security measures.

The hospital's director of security when the shooting occurred testified that the security company had served its limited function well, but he did not want its input on security policies and day-to-day procedures. That was his job and he only needed an outside contractor to supplement the existing program. The hospital director said that he preferred to hire in-house guards whose training he could control and who were more adept at handling the needs of patients and their families. He said he only maintained a contract with the security company to assist him in times of personnel. The security company was only in the picture to provide ancillary services that were not enormously consequential to the security program as a whole. Case closed? Not quite. Enter the expert witness.

The security company had presented a very compelling case that it was not the desire of the customer to receive a comprehensive assessment and they quite frankly did not want recommendations on how to secure the pharmacy area and appeared to be taking full responsibility for making sure that the employees were safe. Not a bad place to be in as a defendant, and things certainly could have been worse if the hospital had chosen to shift the blame and join the chorus of those attempting to hold the company responsible for not being more proactive. However, the victim's family countered with their key witness, a security expert who would testify that despite the position of the company, and their customer, the security provider had a much higher duty to fulfill. The expert witness testified that the security company should have been more proactive as a professional security company under contract.

The expert further testified that despite the minimal force that the security company maintained at the hospital, it should have done a full evaluation of the entire property when it initially began providing services at the hospital in 2000 and continued to do so annually. He also testified that the evaluations should have included interviews with employees who had made several complaints to the hospital about a need for security at the pharmacy. In essence, the expert stated very clearly that it was the responsibility of the security company, on its own initiative, to do a thorough and independent assessment of the hospital property and make recommendations in all areas. He further testified that their failure to do so was in itself an act of negligence.

To summarize each side in this legal conflict, let's review the main points.

Plaintiff

- *There was inadequate security in place to protect the employee from physical harm. The security company knew, or should have known, that this homicide was foreseeable based on past complaints from employees in the pharmacy area, and actual violence committed by the perpetrator.*
- *That on the day the homicide occurred, there were no security measures in place to detect, deter, or prevent it from happening.*
- *It was the independent duty of the security company to evaluate the entire hospital property for security vulnerabilities, and offer actual recommendations for mitigating the vulnerabilities – even in areas in which they were not assigned.*

Defendant

- *The security company was only hired to supplement the internal security force, and their role consistently declined until they were relegated to parking lot duties by the time of the homicide.*
- *The security company had performed annual assessments, but they did not include the pharmacy area in the scope of study, and in*

essence, the assessments were actually done more for marketing purposes than with the intent to improve other areas of the hospital environment.

■ *The customer themselves testified that they did not need, nor did they desire, any recommendations from the security company. They further testified that the security company did a satisfactory job in performing their services, and did not have any noticeable deficiencies.*

While there were certainly some weaknesses in the security company's case (labeling security assessments as "marketing tools" may be one), overall it appears that the liability should lie elsewhere. But turning mainly only expert witness testimony, the security company would not get the benefit of the doubt in this particular case. The jury found that the security company was at fault and awarded $1.5 million to the family of the deceased.

Cases such as this can highlight the need for preparing yourself for future litigation based on the lessons learned from other cases. Internal policies and procedures, and how security companies communicate their services, are very critical components of future litigation strategies. After the final gavel comes down, there is still work to do to make sure you're not in the same position twice.

Case closed: where do I go from here?

It has often been said that some good can come out of every bad situation. In every problem there is a series of solutions waiting to be found. I could go on with a series of positive quotes about how even the darkest times will ultimately give way to the light, but if you were to ask the person who recently endured the long and stressful process of being a defendant in a lawsuit, I'm sure they would struggle to find any positive aspect they could cling to. Win or lose, it is extremely difficult to find any forward moving momentum coming out of litigation. After a trial, you may be burdened with worries over anticipated appeals, or you may be dealing with the reality of legal expenses or the payment of judgments. Just as with any experience in life, the lessons we can learn from court battles, or cases in general, are not only valuable because they teach us that we do not want to repeat the process, but they can also serve as a springboard to make our businesses stronger.

You must be prepared for changes that may occur as the result of a lawsuit. Some can be driven by the customer. I recently experienced an abrupt change that while trivial, illustrated how swift a response can be when lawsuits become a reality. After receiving word that a major accident had occurred on the client's property, I began the process of reaching out to their executive management to offer our assistance and coordinate our efforts. The facts surrounding the accident did not immediately suggest that we were directly involved in the incident, but I always feel that we are an indispensable party because of the role we play at each location and should be ready to assist. In this particular case, there still was, no matter how distant, a real possibility that our company could be inserted into a future legal matter or pulled into any action by virtue of our safety responsibilities at the property. Several years prior to this accident, and in recognition of the great partnership our two companies enjoyed, and specifically to make our employees feel a part of the customer's overall environment, they made the decision to have the security officers wear uniform shirts emblazoned with the customer's name and logo. While this is not always advisable because of employment law issues (see previous discussion on joint employment), it did not seem to be too radical at the time. But once the customer's counsel arrived on the property to investigate the accident, it no longer seemed like such a good idea. After receiving a series of phone calls and a very direct request to make the change, our officers were back in their old uniforms in a matter of hours.

In the aftermath of a legal case, it is advisable to take the opportunity to analyze your business practices and internal policies to see what can be improved. I often hear of a persistent legal myth that has convinced some into believing that any steps taken to improve or change policies and procedures will somehow indicate guilt in a prior incident, or a pending case. I have heard this many times when urging managers to make things better by correcting deficiencies that may have been identified by someone bringing an action against our company, or even a competitor. The logic of this argument suggests that if we change a policy or procedure, or even a physical defect on the property, then that will be a full-blown admission that something was wrong in the first place.[1] While there are legal rules of evidence designed and created for the very purpose of encouraging parties to make needed corrections without fear of it being used against them, this line of reasoning can sometimes cause companies to dig in their heels and refuse to make any changes after experiencing a claim or a lawsuit. In my opinion, they miss a great opportunity to make things better and possibly to prevent future actions.

For a brief period in my career I held the title of Quality Assurance Manager for our company. Part of my duties consisted of ensuring that our policies, procedures, and internal processes were sound, and to see that they were also being followed in every aspect of our operations. I would often find myself attempting to correct identified problems that would present challenges to our ultimate goal of serving our customers and employees effectively. I learned many valuable lessons in that role, but the main one that I still carry with me today is the concept of eliminating the root cause of the problem, not just fixing the consequences. Our natural tendency as business professionals is to identify the consequences of a problem and get it fixed. That is often where the process ends. I still recall an occasion where I was assisting a local manager who was dealing with continual payroll issues.

---

[1] This is known as a Subsequent Remedial Measure and is not typically admissible purely to show that the security company or customer is guilty just because they made a change after the incident. When measures are taken that would have made an earlier injury or harm less likely to occur, evidence of the subsequent measures is not admissible to prove: negligence; culpable conduct; a defect in a product or its design; or a need for a warning or instruction. But the court may admit this evidence for another purpose, such as impeachment or – if disputed – proving ownership, control, or the feasibility of precautionary measures.

This was at a time before the advanced and automated software technology that we enjoy today that theoretically eliminates the chance for any payday errors. During this time there was much more human input, and of course more opportunity to make mistakes. I became involved because the frequency of payroll inaccuracies had reached a critical stage. The management employee who was responsible for the situation was an intelligent and reasonably experienced security professional. But during our first meeting to discuss the matter it became very apparent to me that the reason the problem persisted was simple: he was spending all of his energy and time correcting mistakes, not finding out why they had occurred in the first place. He was content to utilize the system of correcting the payroll errors week after week, when he should have been addressing the root cause that resulted in employees being paid incorrectly.

Often we look at lawsuits as just a "consequence" that needs to be corrected by settling or winning. We never go back and look at some of the root causes and the potential solutions that may be available. This is not to suggest that a lawsuit automatically means that your operations are being conducted in a negligent or haphazard manner, or that you must totally redesign your company from top to bottom just because you have been sued. But I firmly believe that there are many areas that can be, and should be, analyzed and addressed in the aftermath of a lawsuit. Legal cases are draining emotionally and financially, by being prepared for the next one and learning lessons from the last one, you can lessen the strain and make it much more difficult for the next plaintiff to be successful. The following areas should be reviewed, and if needed addressed, at the conclusion of every case.

CONTRACTS

We have spent a fair amount of time covering how critical the contract is in the grand scheme of security litigation, and it should continue to be a prominent discussion topic after the case is closed. How judges, juries, and insurance professionals view your standard contract (or the one you were asked to sign by a customer) is valuable information to be used in the future. Depending on the outcome of a case, you will likely be left with the knowledge of how strong or weak your legal protections are as interpreted by legal contract rules, and there is no better time to re-evaluate what needs to be addressed.

One obvious area of potential revision is the indemnification obligation under your existing contracts. You may still be reeling from shock after experiencing what these clauses really mean and the power they can possess. I have spoken to many security professionals who have had an abrupt education on what is actually contained in the endless documents that we are asked to sign. Many did not previously realize the dynamics of having to "cover" someone else when a lawsuit happens, or how they could be pulled into an action that they otherwise had no real connection to.

This is a decision that often will rest more on business philosophy regarding how much risk you are willing to absorb, than it will on actual legal theory, but in the afterglow of litigation you can usually see more clearly what the risks are. Take that knowledge and build upon it to limit risks in the future.

Some basic review areas in regard to indemnification provisions found in your standard contract, and customer contracts you are asked to sign, should include:

- *Does the contract include not only an indemnity obligation but also hold harmless and an express duty to defend clause?*
- *Are the indemnitee's legal fees and costs of defense included within the scope of indemnity?*
- *Are the types of claims identified? (Third Party Claims, bodily injury or death, etc.)*
- *Who are you required to cover? (Customer's affiliates, officers, directors, employees, agents, contractors, etc.)*
- *Is my duty to indemnify limited to the security company's own negligence, or does it encompass acts committed by the customer?*
- *Beware of "in connection with" or "arising out of" language as this may be broadly construed and connect the obligation with a variety of potential claims.*
- *Is the indemnity clause consistent with my current insurance coverage, and other contractual clauses?*

Another area of contract review should be the description of roles and responsibilities. Many times litigation will center on who was ultimately responsible for making important decisions concerning vital security functions such as staffing, post locations, and post instructions. Considerations such as including language in your contract identifying these responsibilities should be discussed and possible approaches analyzed. You may want to consider documenting the response of the customer to the offer of an assessment within the body of the contract, and/or clearly outlining the duties that will be required of the officers once both parties agree what they are.

The days following a lawsuit can also be filled with thoughts of what more can, or needs, to be done to sufficiently protect the customer. You may even find yourself in the position of having to deal with new rules or contractual language imposed by the customer as a direct result of the legal action. I have witnessed this several times. After an indemnification action several years ago, we were coming up on the time for contract renewal and I was presented with a new agreement to be signed. A quick check of the old agreement revealed that the case we were just a part of had prompted a new philosophy on how to handle the issue of indemnification and hold harmless. We did not make new law, but we definitely gave birth to a new contract.

Another unique episode played out in a similar context. As happens from time to time, thankfully very rarely, a customer experienced a loss that while not directly tied to our services, did result in filing an insurance claim with our carrier. After a thorough investigation, the decision was made by our insurance carrier that we were not the responsible party and were not obligated to cover the loss. We had a very close relationship with the customer, and thankfully the matter did not have a substantial impact on our ability to continue to provide our services.

About a month or so later, I was visiting the customer location and was meeting with our customer representative. After some additional discussions about the state of our services and plans for future growth, he mentioned the claim denial and asked for further clarification. The conversation was extremely cordial and positive, and I was more than willing to explain to him the process that was undertaken and how it ultimately led to the decision not to reimburse them for the loss. He seemed very appreciative of my explanation and again showed no signs that the matter would come between us professionally. But at the end of our meeting he did make what I considered to be a somewhat unusual request.

He began to inquire as to whether or not there was a contractual remedy that would prevent our insurance company from denying these types of claims in the future. I responded that while every situation is unique and lends itself to certain interpretations based on the contractual language in effect at the time and other factors, placing new or different wording in the agreement could conceivably alter future claim decisions. I then gave the standard response of advising him to consult with his counsel to see what would be the best approach to achieve this goal. It was at this point that he made a somewhat surprising request. He asked if I would be willing to draft the necessary language to be inserted into our agreement for the purpose of broadening our scope of liability, specifically in the area we had just experienced. This being a loyal, and by the way large customer, I felt obliged to offer my service if he felt it was warranted. But I must admit it did feel like I was being asked to bet against the home team. But once again, that is the real world, and it doesn't always line up perfectly with the legal universe.

Another area of review after a lawsuit should be what type of business you are targeting in your marketing efforts and ultimately accepting as customers. There is risk in every contract security environment, and you will never find an ideal client that comes with any guarantee of never having to face litigation. But, working in some customer environments can bring more risk than others, and while this is a purely business decision, take the time to evaluate if the services you are providing in certain environments are worth the financial benefit.

MARKETING MATERIALS

Like any business, security companies have the need to make sure that potential customers know about their products and services. Getting the word out is increasingly important as competition increases and there are a multitude of companies vying for the chance to get their foot in the door and a chance of landing the next big account. This is done in a variety of ways. Marketing brochures and websites are still staples in any sales plan and provide a way for the security company to communicate how their products and services can assist the customer with their overall security needs, and what qualifications the company has to be a competent provider. I certainly don't see a time where companies will decide to stop marketing their services just to counteract any fears of potential lawsuits, but you should be aware of what impact they can have if one arises.

Marketing materials can be subject to discovery and can be a valuable weapon in the hands of a skilled plaintiff's attorney. They are sought after to show what the company was claiming they could accomplish through their services and will be used to establish that the company knew it that it had certain responsibilities to safe guard a property because that's what it promised to do in its marketing material. This can even include specific proposals to the customer who may now be the focus of litigation.

In almost every case I have been involved in relating to negligent security, at some point the documents that formed an offer or proposal for services was brought up in depositions, or in pleadings. And often seemingly innocuous words or statements can take on a larger meaning. If certain service "promises" are made in the proposal, you can expect to have to answer for how it was, or was not, carried out later on. These can include security assessments, post order creation, and officer training and qualifications. A recent case filed against one of the largest electronic security companies in the country illustrates how marketing images can be used to attack a company over perceived false claims.

In a class action filed in 2014, a series of plaintiffs allege, among other things, that a provider of security alarm services has mislead the consumer by offering a sense of security in their marketing communications that don't match reality.[2] Some of the marketing languages mentioned specifically in the lawsuit are: "Get Security You Can Count On. Every Day of the Year" and "Your haven is armed with 24-hour-a-day protection, 365 days a year."[3] Phrases such as this are being used in this lawsuit in an attempt to show that reality does not match what is being promised. I have seen similar scenarios play out in security officer cases.

On more than one occasion I have found myself being interrogated by a plaintiff's attorney over how our actual services matched up to what is promised in our brochures and proposals. There is no magical solution for getting this to stop all together, but there are steps you can take to avoid its impact. First, is what you are saying in your marketing materials accurate and defendable? Does it cross a line from marketing fluff into false expectations? Examine your marketing language to see, from an objective standpoint, if it could be misconstrued at a later date to place unreasonable expectations in the mind of a customer, or even a jury. Be careful using words such as "always" and "guarantee" as this may appear to suggest that your services are designed to prevent anything from ever happening, and of course no one guarantee that.

Another area of concern can be the use of standard proposal formats. Virtually every company has a predesigned proposal that is used to communicate offers to prospects. There is nothing inherently wrong with utilizing a standard format, and it would be unreasonable to suggest that a new proposal must be created from scratch every time a prospective customer contact is made, but there are some areas to be aware of.

I once found myself in the midst of a case involving an injured party where I was being forced to painstakingly explain virtually every aspect of our standard proposal. Almost every sentence that could somehow have been construed as a promise or proposed obligation was being scrutinized. In regards to the case we were trying, the post orders were a central item, and in this case the customer – at their insistence – had created them without any assistance from our company. But our proposal contained a sentence at that time that read in part; "(Security Company) will become familiar with the security needs of (customer) and will create a comprehensive set of post instructions to be followed by security personnel …." A simple and fairly innocent statement, but in light the pending legal dispute, it became a point of contention.

---

[2]Dale Baker v. The ADT Corporation, IN THE UNITED STATES DISTRICT COURT FOR THE NORTHERN DISTRICT OF ILLINOIS. Case No.: No. 14 cv 8988 (2014).
[3]This case dealt primarily with the defendant's alleged inability to prevent attempts to hack into their secure network.

While it was undisputed, at least in my mind, that we had played no real role in creating the instructions, this simple "promise" contained in our proposal gave the other side a leverage point that was causing me to reluctantly admit that we did not always follow exactly the words contained in our own literature, which of course opened the door to questioning whether or not we did anything we promised. In this situation, the simple addition of "where applicable" or "upon request" to the sentence would likely have shut down that line of questioning and the necessity of having to explain repeatedly that I did not have a set of post instructions hidden somewhere that our company had created but failed to share with the customer, or the plaintiff during discovery.

After a lawsuit, take the time to evaluate your marketing materials based on lessons you have learned, and how they could be viewed in future actions. No reason to toss everything out, but you may find something that could easily be fixed before it becomes a vulnerability in the future.

INSURANCE COVERAGE

Allow me to dispense with the obvious before we go any further, after a lawsuit is not the ideal time to figure out if you have adequate insurance coverage. Those discussions, of course, should happen well before you experience a major loss. But I believe this is very much an evolutionary process and should be reviewed on a periodic basis. Matters such as policy limits, aggregates, and other factors should be evaluated at least annually to make sure the company is not unnecessarily exposed.

It is also prudent to take a step back and examine the overall role the insurance carrier and broker played in the life of a case. Based on my experience, they play a vital part in its success or failure. There is something very comforting about getting something as negative and troubling as a lawsuit into the hands of an experienced insurance professional who knows how to navigate the troubling waters that lay ahead.

Seemingly simple matters can also be overlooked when purchasing insurance, or reviewing policies after a legal action has been filed. Many companies are not adequately insured because they are unaware of the distinction between two different types of liability insurance. Legal costs can quickly exhaust your policy limit leaving you to pay out of pocket for claims or settlements. There are differences that all security companies should be aware of in order to make sure they have the proper coverage.

"Defense inside the limit" means that all defense costs (attorney's fees, court costs, and investigation and filing legal papers) are deducted first from the policy limit, which cuts into the overall limit of dollars available to pay for monetary damages awarded by a ruling. For example, if you have $1 million in coverage, but the policy states that defense costs are inside the limits, you could very easily reach your limit in attorney's fees and costs and have nothing left over to pay judgments. This is a critical distinction. In contrast, with "outside the limit coverage," there are separate limits available for legal defense costs and court-awarded damages. So, the cost of defending your case does not erode your policy limits available to pay settlements resulting from a lawsuit. Knowing what types of coverage you have is critical before the lawsuit comes, but certainly should be reviewed after you have been sued.

This is also an opportune time to plan for additional limits and other policy considerations that may be a direct reflection of your experiences in a legal case. Make certain you work with insurance professionals that specialize in the security services industry as they have a unique perspective on the risks we face and how our industry operates. You may find less expensive coverage from other carriers, but I can assure you that the extra investment will be worth it when the battle lines are drawn.

POST ORDERS/INSTRUCTIONS

It is a rare security-related loss that does not prominently feature at some point the instructions that were given to the officers detailing what responsibilities were expected to be fulfilled, and the desired result. Unfortunately, many times in our industry this is another area that has fallen prey to the quick and easy boilerplate solution. A recent experience with security ligation can highlight the need to review all post instructions at each location. Taking the time to examine any vulnerabilities will prepare you for the next event.

Post instructions can neither cover every conceivable potential security event, nor can they effectively outline every potential response to each. I'm sure many well-meaning plaintiff attorneys would argue with this assessment, but it is not reasonable to assume the post orders can give a quick and simple solution to every possible bad thing that could happen at a particular site. But they should reflect the overall mission of the security plan, and the steps that should be taken to achieve that goal.

Particular attention should be given to the following areas in post instructions:

- *Post Locations:* Is it clear as to where the officers should be stationed? Security office? Patrol?
- *Duties:* Are the duties clearly spelled out? For example, do the post orders simply say "front gate officer should control access to the

facility" or do they actually spell out how this is to be accomplished? In addition, are conflicts in the duties clearly identified? Is the officer who is required to control front gate access, also required to perform patrol rounds? If so, how is access controlled during that time?

- *Chronology:* Many post instructions will lay out a long list of duties according to a time chart. While these may be helpful to assist the officer in knowing when and where to be, they also should be evaluated to ensure they are accurate based on current procedures and analyzed to see if they are realistic in the actual environment.

- *Response Required:* Many take for granted this aspect of post orders but outlining the proper response security officers should take in reaction to a particular incident can be crucial depending on the nature of the claim. It is assumed that the proper response for all crimes in progress will be to notify law enforcement, but what about other types of incidents? Often product loss claims turn on whether or not the security officer notified the proper party. I've been involved in cases where this is either omitted from the post orders, or at minimum ambiguous or confusing. This will likely be the standard that your insurance company will use to accept or deny the claim. So making it is as clear as possible could save you and your customer time and financial trouble.

In addition to these areas, the more general problem of relevancy can be concerning. It is always disheartening to read a deposition transcript of a security professional who is being quizzed on the contents of post instructions and their only answer is to repeat the phrase "we don't do that any longer" over and over in response to why certain procedures were not followed. I recently was engaged to perform some consulting work that included a review of a customer's emergency procedures. I was given several very detailed and organized volumes that contained policies and plans on a variety of areas such as chemical spills and bomb threat response. After each plan description, a roster of employees who made up the response team for each potential event was listed. Upon further inquiry, I learned that most of the employees listed either no longer worked there, had retired, and some were even deceased. Great plans, but because they were not up to date, they would likely not have been very effective.

Post instructions should be annually reviewed and updated if necessary. This is also an excellent time to sit down with the customer and discuss the overall mission and what duties are most relevant. This will not only serve as a mechanism to make your business and the service you provide to our customer stronger, but it will assist you in presenting a much better case should future litigation arise. It is never a positive visual when a security company produces an endless stream of memos, handwritten notes, emails, or other unorganized forms of documentation, purporting to be the "post orders" for a particular site. Taking the time to review and update the instructions will serve you well in future.

ASSESSMENT METHODOLOGY

Nothing reinforces the notion that those involved in the security profession are truly expected to be experts, then the experience of a lawsuit. It is an abrupt reminder that we are looked at to provide guidance, advice, and ultimately competent services to meet the needs of our customers. Some attempt to run from this label, especially when it is becoming apparent that a high legal standard comes along with it. After several of my speaking engagements over the years, I have been approached by some in the industry who have told me that in response to fears of legal liability, they no longer even use the word "security" to describe what they do, and have invented alternative labels with the hope that when push comes to legal shove they can escape from any consequences by claiming that they were never in the security business to begin with. It is not my place to be critical of any single business preferences or liability philosophies, as we each have to make the decisions we feel are best for our companies. But as an industry, with all of its evolving needs and challenges, we must continue to rise to the occasion. We can either run to meet the challenge of being an expert, or away from it.

How we go about the process of advising our clients is critical to our professional reputation, but is also important in the area of legal liability. After the case is closed, many lessons can be learned in regards to what our role is when advising our client on best practices to combat their security challenges. This is one area that you will consistently struggle with as you deal with some customers who have no need or desire for advice, and others who may be solely dependent upon your guidance to effectively construct a security program. A successful security professional will be able to deal effectively with both.

The issue of assessments and recommendations should be on the table as early as possible in the relationship. Knowing what the customer expects, and what can be done to meet those expectations, is critical. Don't wait until a major event occurs in order to use hindsight to apply proven techniques. And beyond just the initial assessment, continual evaluations are necessary to make sure the program responds to evolving threats and conditions.

Experiences in litigation can refocus our efforts on our role and responsibility in the area of providing assessment services. Consider the following questions as you find your company's identity in this area:

- *From a company wide perspective, how involved are we in establishing security policies and procedures at the site level?*
- *Do we allow our customers to create the majority of all security measures at the sites we service?*
- *Do our customers have any awareness of our potential legal responsibility to alert them of any perceived vulnerabilities and offer recommendations?*
- *Is a site assessment done for all new customers? If so, is the site assessment documented and shared with the customer prior to commencing service?*
- *Is an annual assessment performed, and if so, is the scope discussed with the customer prior to performing?*
- *Are results from the annual assessment shared with the customer?*

Performing assessments can be delicate as many customers will not wholeheartedly embrace the process, but this is a vital link in the security services chain, and will rear its head in future cases. Having a company plan and roadmap in this area will serve you well before the next suit comes.

OFFICER SELECTION/TRAINING PROGRAMS

It is hard to pinpoint one single area as being the most important aspect of successfully defending security litigation, but the issue of officer selection and training comes very close. This one issue can impact your ability to offer any meaningful legal theories that you were performing as you were required to. The question of officer competency is not just necessary to make certain that you are effectively serving your customers, it can be the difference in maintaining your survival in litigation.

At the end of the day, we are in the people business. Officers are not just what we do, they are who we are. If we fail in that regard, we don't have much hope to succeed in other areas. While I don't ordinarily perform duties on a post as a regular part of my job, I never lose sight of the fact that the point at which the service is provided trumps everything else. Regardless of what we tell ourselves, the reality is that what the security officer does day-in and day-out is far more important and vital than any other role in the company. We should make certain that we are devoting our energy and resources in this area accordingly.

The process you follow to screen, hire, and train your employees will be under a virtual microscope in a security lawsuit. Every step you take, or did not take, will be examined in an effort to prove that you had the wrong person for the job, or they were not prepared properly to assume the duties. As I have often said when training managers, don't follow our screening, hiring, and training process just to shield us from lawsuits, do it so we can have the best people possible representing our company and our customers. But having effective cover in a lawsuit is a nice by-product.

I have read many cases that were won or lost on simple aspects such as the amount of training the officer received, or the failure to conduct an adequate background check. Have a solid policy and follow it consistently.

Here are some steps related to screening, hiring, and training for review:

OFFICER SCREENING

Does your process consistently involve the following prehire steps:

- Criminal History Check[4]
- Employment History Check
- Educations History Check
- Personal References
- Preemployment Drug Testing
- Extensive Interview
- Licensed by the State according to current regulations

TRAINING (INITIAL AND ONGOING)

Does your employee-training program, at minimum, include the following:

- Patrol Techniques
- Report Writing
- Access Control
- Emergency Response
- Civil Powers to Arrest
- Employee Safety
- CPR/First Aid
- Responding to Crimes
- Dealing with Aggressive or Violent Persons
- Reporting Suspicious Activity
- Postspecific Duties

---

[4]Many states and municipalities have enacted laws making it illegal to ask certain questions concerning criminal history during the prehire phase. Check the laws in your state of operation for guidance prior to any inquiry.

When I explain security litigation, or litigation in general, I have often remarked that facts are initially born as assumptions. While that sounds like inverted logic, I have seen it play out time and time again. If a security officer has a less than stellar background, one will assume that he was not an effective deterrent or did not provide an appropriate response to the event in question. If training was lacking, it will be assumed that the officer was not properly equipped to deal with the event that has now caused a loss or great harm to an individual. Neither of these "assumptions" may be entirely factual, but strong inferences can, and will, be drawn from them if proper procedures are not followed. I have seen many cases where the security officer did exactly what he or she should have done, but due to the fact that there were obvious problems in the hiring or training process, the entire episode is tainted with doubt.

One of your main goals in litigation should be to avoid spending endless hours explaining why screening was not a priority, or why the training program lacked certain elements. Invest the time now to make sure they are as strong as they can be, so in the future you will have a solid foundation to stand upon when the questions come.

CONCLUSIONS

As I reach the end of this book, I hope that I have imparted through my experiences, the positive and negative ones, some sense of what to expect when litigation comes, and more importantly how to prepare for it and react to it. Unfortunately, we practice a profession that is prone to legal actions, and I only expect that to intensify in the coming years. I hope this work will serve as a volume of information that you can refer to when you find yourself in the crosshairs of a legal action. Being educated on what to expect and how to respond is not only an issue to consider, it is the issue, when dealing with security litigation. All is never lost when you are armed with knowledge about what is coming. Hopefully through these pages you've found something to make yourself a much harder target to hit when the plaintiff comes. If just one company is able to better prepare for litigation, or respond to it, the goal of writing this book will have been achieved.

Appendices

As an example and a quick reference guide, I have included several sample documents and checklists essential in the area of security litigation. While they will provide guidance on certain topics and issues, you should always consult with legal counsel prior to implementing any new policy or using any new contractual agreements.

For all applicable appendices ABC Security Company is utilized as a fictional placeholder.

APPENDIX A
SAMPLE SECURITY SERVICES AGREEMENT

The following is an example of a basic security services agreement. It contains provisions covering operational and legal matters. It is provided as an example and reference to be utilized when constructing your own agreement, and provides increased protection for security providers. Due to variations in state laws, customer preferences, insurance coverage, and risk assumption philosophy, security companies should have any agreement reviewed by an attorney prior to utilizing it in the ordinary course of business.

SECURITY SERVICES AGREEMENT

THIS AGREEMENT made on the _____ day of _____ in the year of _____, as between ABC Security Services, a corporation organized under the laws of the State of (hereinafter referred to as "ABC") and _____ (hereinafter referred to as "the Customer").

1. Job Site Address:
   ABC shall furnish the Customer uniformed security service as required by the Customer at the following address, and at any other location(s) as requested by the customer.

Name
Street Address
City, State, Zip
Contact Name/Title

   Service shall commence on _____, and shall continue until cancelled as herein provided. This Agreement, and all terms herein, may not be amended or modified in whole or in part, except by a writing specifically referring to the portion or portions of this Agreement to be amended or modified and executed by the parties hereto.

1. Weekly Hours of Service
   Weekly hours of Service: _____. These hours will be deemed "normal." Normal hours can be changed upon seven (7) days' written notice.
2. Duties
   It is hereby acknowledged that the customer is solely responsible for determining the set number of service hours per week and is also solely

responsible for issuing orders governing the security functions of the officers on duty.

In the alternative, the security company is willing to conduct a security assessment analyzing the customer's property and offering recommendations in regard to number of weekly hours, post locations, and security duties.

Customer herby

_____ accepts Security Company's offer of a security assessment
Customer Initials: _____

_____ rejects Security Company's offer of a security assessment
Customer Initials: _____

The security company (Company) shall provide services, as more fully described in Exhibit "A" attached hereto and made a part hereof (collectively, the "Work"), in accordance with the terms and conditions set forth herein. The Work generally consists of on-site security guard services at the Customer's facility located at 123 Elm Street New York, NY (the "Site"). All security officers will be licensed according to the current jurisdictional regulations and will be UNARMED. The Service shall commence on January 1, 2016.

Weekly Hours of Service: Weekly hours of Service: 168. These hours will be deemed "normal." Normal hours can be changed upon one (1) day's written notice to the company.

3. Billing/Pay Rates

Wage	Straight Time	Billing Rate	Overtime Billing Rate
_____	_____	_____	_____

Other Charges:	$_____	$_____	$_____	$_____
	Radio/Phone	Tour System	Vehicle	Other

Overtime will only be billed with the approval of the Customer; however, in the event that abnormally bad weather conditions and/ or natural disasters create road conditions that prevent our personnel from getting to or from their posts, the overtime incurred by ABC for officers stranded on the job (in a working status) and the overtime for replacement officers filling posts when the normally assigned officer is stranded at home or in his/her community shall be billable to the Customer.

The Customer agrees that ABC is authorized to adjust billing rates for any increase in costs caused by government-mandated increases in wages, benefits, or payroll-based taxes. Any increase in cost will be accounted for in, and become a part of each periodic bill.

4. Payment Terms

    ABC will bill the Customer _____ Weekly _____Monthly. Payment shall be made by the Customer to ABC without discount, not later than thirty (30) days after the date of billing. Past due accounts shall bear a service charge of the lesser of 2% per month or the legal maximum rate allowed. Modification to this Agreement may require changes in the quoted prices.

5. Employees

    a. All security officers furnished by ABC will be the employees of ABC. ABC will have the sole responsibility to pay the wages, taxes (including but not limited to Social Security and Federal and State Unemployment Taxes) and all other expenses relating to each employee of ABC. ABC shall be responsible for the hiring, training, and supervision of such employees.

    b. Notwithstanding any other provision in this agreement, and because the Customer has sole control over the condition of its premises, the Customer warrants and represents that it will provide and maintain safe working conditions for ABC personnel.

    c. ABC employees will be assigned to the Customer's facility without regard to race, color, age, creed, national origin, gender, or any other status for which employees are protected by Federal, State, or Municipal law.

6. Hiring

    It is agreed that ABC is not an employment agency and the security officers it furnishes are made possible only by a substantial investment in advertising, recruiting, testing, and training of the personnel. In consideration of the time and expense invested in these security officers, it is agreed that the Customer will not hire any security officer from ABC while the security officer is still employed by ABC, or for ninety (90) days after termination of the security officer from ABC. The Customer agrees to pay a placement fee of $1000 for every ABC employee whom the Customer hires in violation of this agreement.

7. Liabilities and Indemnities

    a. The Customer agrees that ABC is not an insurer and the amounts payable hereunder are based on the value of services offered and not the value of the Customer's interests being protected, or the potential for loss of property. ABC does not guarantee or promise that a loss will not occur. ABC undertakes no liability to the Customer and makes no representation, express or implied, that its services will prevent occurrences or their consequences that result in loss or damage.

b. The Customer shall indemnify and hold harmless ABC, its agents, and employees (hereinafter referred to collectively in the singular as "Indemnitee") from and against any loss, damage, injury, liability, claim, demand, or lien (including the payment of all damages, expenses, costs, and attorney's fees) for injury to person or property or death of a person, including injury to or death of the Customer's agents or employees, resulting from the negligence, or willful misconduct of the Customer, or its agents or employees, or a dangerous or defective condition on the premises, or for any strict liability or liability without fault which is imposed on or sought to be imposed on the Customer, its agents or employees. The Customer shall not indemnify and hold harmless the Indemnitee from and against any loss, damage, injury, liability, claim, or lien for injury to person or property or death of any person resulting from the negligence or willful misconduct of the Indemnitee. ABC shall notify the Customer promptly or any known written claims or demands against it in connection herewith. The Customer agrees to indemnify and hold harmless ABC and its employees, from any and all loss, damage, injury liability, claim, or cause of action for injury to person or property arising out of the detention of any person by ABC employees upon direction of the Customer, except for such loss, death, or injuries occasioned by the willful misconduct or negligence of the said employee in detaining a suspect. ABC shall indemnify and hold harmless the Customer, its agents and employees (hereinafter referred to collectively in the singular as "Indemnitee") from and against any loss, damage, injury liability, claim or lien for injury to person or property, or death of a person, resulting from the sole negligence or willful misconduct of ABC's in the performance of ABC's work herein. ABC shall not indemnify and hold harmless the Indemnitee from and against any loss, damage, injury, liability, claim, or lien for injury to person or property, or death of any such person resulting from the negligence or willful misconduct of the Indemnitee or defect on the premises, or for any strict liability or liability without fault which is imposed on or sought to be imposed on the Indemnitee. The Customer shall notify ABC promptly of any known written claims or demands against it in connection herewith.

c. The Customer agrees to indemnify and hold harmless ABC and its employees, from any claims of discrimination based on race, color, national origin, sex, age, religion, or disability arising from acts performed by ABC employees pursuant to the directions of the Customer, except for such claims of discrimination occasioned by the willful misconduct or sole negligence of said ABC employee. The right of indemnity herein shall include the provision of a defense in any action pertaining to a claim of discrimination and payment of all costs, judgments, or settlements in connection therewith.

d. The Customer hereby waives any and all rights of subrogation that any insurer of Customer may have against ABC.

8. Force *Majure*

The obligations of ABC hereunder may be suspended during any period where performance is prevented by acts of God, civil or labor disturbances, or events beyond ABC's reasonable control.

9. Insurance

a. ABC maintains, for its own protection, general liability, automobile liability, and employee fidelity coverage.

b. The Customer agrees to assume all risks of loss or damage to its premises occurring as a result of fire, theft, or other casualty and the Customer agrees that it will maintain insurance to fully protect the Customer against such damage.

10. Cancellation

Either party may cancel this Agreement at any time upon thirty (30) days' written notice by Certified Mail. Notice for Company under this agreement shall be sent to _____. Notice for Customer may be sent to _____. The date the notice is postmarked shall serve as the beginning of the 30-day notice period.

11. Default

a. Notwithstanding any other provisions of this agreement, ABC may terminate this agreement immediately, without notice, and exercise such other rights and remedies as permitted by law, if the Customer fails to pay any amount due or if any proceeding is commenced or threatened against the Customer under the Bankruptcy Code or any other Debtor's law, or if the Customer makes, or threatens to make, an assignment for the benefits of creditors.

b. In the event that the Customer shall default and ABC shall deem it necessary to refer its claim for collection from the Customer to its attorneys, the Customer acknowledges that all payments due under this Agreement are payable in _____, and therefore, the venue for any action filed by ABC for collection of the said payments shall be in _____. The Customer also agrees to pay any and all reasonable attorneys fees and the costs incurred by ABC in the process of collecting past due amounts.

12. Entire Agreement and Interpretation

This Agreement constitutes the entire Agreement and understanding between the parties. This Agreement shall be enforced under the laws of the state of Alabama. The Agreement may not be modified orally, but only in writing signed by the parties hereto. Any failure by ABC at any time, or from time to time, to enforce or require the strict keeping and performance of any of the terms of this Agreement, or to exercise a right hereunder, shall not constitute a waiver of, and shall not affect the right of ABC at any time to avail itself of same. If there is a discrepancy between any document and the Agreement, then the Agreement and any attachment or addendum thereto shall govern. If there is a discrepancy between the Agreement and any other document comprising part of or attached to the Agreement, then the Agreement shall govern. This Agreement shall be binding upon successors, assigns, or transferees of the Customer.

ABC SECURITY SERVICES: _____ CUSTOMER: _____

Signature: _____ Signature: _____

Print Name: _____ Print Name: _____

Title: _____ Title: _____

APPENDIX B

INTERNAL CHECKLIST FOR CUSTOMER CONTRACTS

In order to properly evaluate the terms and conditions of a security services agreement, certain data is required. Operational aspects such as the duties that the officer will be expected to perform, and the results of any completed risk assessments, must be taken into account.

The following is a sample internal checklist to be used by salespersons or field managers when submitting a proposed contract for review.

CONTRACT REVIEW CHECKLIST

Contract Name: _____

Date Submitted: _____ Submitted by:_____

Bill Rate: _____ Pay Rate: _____

1. Is Company currently providing service for this customer? YES   NO

   If yes, what date was service started: _____

   If no, what is the anticipated start date: _____

2. List amount of coverage under this contract: _____HPW (hours per week).

ARMED   UNARMED (circle one)

3. Has customer provided Company with post orders or any other operating instructions?

    YES   NO

    If yes, please attach a copy of orders.

4. Has a security assessment been performed and submitted to customer?

    YES   NO

5. Will Officers be expected to drive customer-owned vehicles?   YES   NO

6. Will Officers be expected to drive Company-owned vehicles?   YES   NO

7. Please list the following equipment that Company has agreed to provide to customer

    (e.g., tour system, radios, cell phones, computers, etc.)

    _____

    _____

    _____

8. Please explain how the items in #7 are being billed (i.e., built into rate, etc.)

    _____

    _____

9. What State will this service be performed in? _____

10. What type of business is customer involved in? _____

APPENDIX C

The following is a basic template of a SECURITY ASSESSMENT performed for a fictional Hospital/Healthcare Customer. The actual content is not included for any purpose other than as a suggested format, and should not be taken as an indication that the recommendations contained herein should be offered as a potential security solution. This is offered as an example of a possible Assessment report template and methodology only.

SECURITY ASSESSMENT

PREPARED FOR:

Hospital Example
Conducted by:

*********************PRIVATE AND CONFIDENTIAL*******************
THE INFORMATION CONTAINED IN THIS ASSESSMENT REPORT IS CONSIDERED PRIVATE AND CONFIDENTIAL.IT SHOULD NOT BE VIEWED BY ANYONE OUTSIDE OF -------------------- . IT IS RECOMMENDED THAT THIS INFORMATION BE SHARED ONLY WITH SENIOR MANAGEMENT AND SUPERVISORY STAFF.

TABLE OF CONTENTS

Active Shooter _____

General Recommendations _____

Summary _____

Introduction

_____, 2015

Dear,

A security assessment was performed for --------------------. The physical assessment was conducted by --------, with the assistance of ---.

In developing the recommendations contained in this report, ABC Security Company has relied on a physical tour of the exterior and interior of the facilities, a review of current security measures and Standard Operating Procedures, as well as responses from brief interactions with the facility personnel. We have provided -------------------- with practical recommendations that we feel will enhance your current security and provide additional protection to your employees, occupants, visitors, and assets. In doing so, we have attempted to address any and all vulnerabilities that were noted during the assessment. However, if you are aware of other areas and/or issues that need to be studied, please feel free to bring this to our attention and we would be more than willing to advise you accordingly.

It should be noted that what is contained in this report is not the result of an exhaustive assessment analyzing all aspects of the current security operations and internal site functions, but rather general recommendations based on an overview of the facilities and data received. The primary areas of focus during our visit were access control, responding to the current threat environment, and physical vulnerabilities.

Proper risk assessments include both an understanding of the threats to the hospital as well as the vulnerabilities that could allow a threat to be carried out. Examples of the threats can range from simple thefts of staff or patients' personal belongings to violent offenses such as an armed attack, sexual assault, or homicide. Each of these can be deterred, and in some cases prevented, by recognizing and mitigating the vulnerabilities that allow the threats to occur.

Some examples of common vulnerabilities in hospitals are inadequate access control, nonexistent or inoperable video systems, or ineffective training in the predictive indicators of aggressive behaviors. Once the threats and vulnerabilities are understood, the next step is to develop appropriate and cost-effective mitigation measures. Depending on the risk, these measures could include lighting, lock systems, video, access control, security staffing, training, and even landscaping. In the following report, you will find more specific findings.

ABC followed a basic Risk Assessment format during the assessment process:

Asset Identification: Common assets in a healthcare environment include patients, staff, visitors, and property. Other less tangible assets include the overall perception of the hospital's security department by the public and staff, and the reputation of the hospital in the community.

Current Security Measures: During this process, ABC evaluated the information provided and the measures personally observed during the on-site visit.

Threat Assessment: As more fully described in the report, healthcare environments have risk that are inherent to all (aggressive behavior in the emergency department, mental health risks, outside criminal elements), but the level of other risks will vary by facility depending on the geographic location, current security measures, and internal dynamics.

Vulnerability Assessment: Through observation of current measures and past incidents, ABC has attempted to highlight all observed security vulnerabilities that should be addressed to prevent any future incidents or losses.

Rick Assessment: While this report does not include an exhaustive cost/benefit analysis (ABC can provide this if or when -------------------- Hospital begins the process of implementing any proposed solution), we have included the reasoning behind implementing such measures and the potential benefit gained by doing so.

We would like to express our appreciation to all -------------------- Team Members for their cooperation during this process, and especially you for taking the time to speak with me about the process. If ABC can ever be of additional assistance, please do not hesitate to call.

Sincerely,

Facility description

-------------------- is a healthcare provider with two main hospital facilities as well as numerous buildings surrounding the main campus that house various departments and clinics. ------------------- Hospital is a ---- bed facility with outpatient, inpatient, Women's Center, and general emergency services.

There is a second location located at ------------------- St, (-------------------) that serves as an acute inpatient/outpatient rehabilitation center.

The hospital is equipped with multiple public entrances during day time hours. The facility is open for general public access until 9:00 PM when the only access point is through the emergency department.

------------------- Hospital Regional currently utilizes a contract security force whose primary duties are to maintain a visible presence and patrol the properties.

Current security staffing structure

According to a review of the current schedule, the security department is staffed with the following personnel on a routine basis.

Insert current staffing schedule

Geographical location/current risk/area crime analysis

The hospital frequently experiences the admission of patients under mental health watch and has experienced patient elopements. The hospital has not experienced a great deal of criminal activity recently. It was noted during the assessment that the Main Campus has been subjected to several vehicle burglaries and occasional internal theft. The issue seems to be more prominent at the ------------------- location due to the surrounding area. The crime in the -------------------Street vicinity is higher, and due to the lack of activity in many areas of the property (vacant buildings), it is desirable to homeless persons and random criminal acts of vandalism and burglary.

Approximately ----cameras are located throughout the property and can be viewed by the security department in the security office. Some cameras are not currently in operation and need to be repaired.

Internal incident reports

In reviewing the internal incident data, and information gathered through interviews with security department employees, it appears that the hospital has experienced the following for the time period -----through ----------:

General observations

The primary goal of a healthcare security force is remaining as visible as possible to serve as a deterrent to criminal activity, and to convey a message of safety to the patients and visitors. This must be accomplished in several ways: maintaining a high profile presence in the various hospital buildings, performing regular and deliberate vehicle patrols, and being continually posted at certain high-risk locations (Emergency Room/Mental Health Areas).

The current security force appears to be doing an adequate job in maintaining high visibility and serving as a deterrent. The following recommendations are offered to increase this effort and enhance the overall security program:

Observation #1: External Patrols

The strongest deterrent to vehicle burglaries, and other criminal activity in parking areas, is a constant presence of a security vehicle. This should include all parking areas, surrounding buildings, and other perimeter locations. -------------------- Hospital security officers are assigned a small vehicle for the purpose of patrolling the hospital property. A golf cart is also available to the security department at certain times. During the assessment, particularly on the evening of March 31, the security vehicle was observed being used to patrol the hospital parking areas. However, due to the vehicle type, and lack of security lighting, the assessor did not immediately recognize the vehicle as belonging to security.

Recommendation #1: Consider a Replacement Patrol Vehicle

Continuous patrols in and around the parking areas and hospital property is essential to maintain visibility, a deterrent effect, and a secure atmosphere. The officer responsible for patrol should be engaging in patrol unless otherwise occupied. This effort is hampered when a vehicle that is not highly visible is utilized. ABC would recommend that consideration be given to a light SUV-type vehicle. The vehicle should be equipped with an amber security light that should be active when the patrols are being performed. The vehicle should also bear clearly visible markings indicating "SECURITY" and other required lettering per ------regulations.

ABC can provide vehicle options and pricing upon your request.

Observation #2: Internal Patrols (Officer Visibility)

In addition to maintaining a high level of visibility in the parking areas and around the perimeter of the hospital property, it is extremely important for the security officers to be seen frequently throughout the interior of the buildings as well.

Recommendation #2: Increase Officer Visibility

As noted above, internal rounds are just as important as external visibility. Along with exterior vehicle patrols, the Officers should be constantly patrolling the interior of the hospital, paying special attention to sensitive areas. ABC recommends that officers be directed to maintain even greater visibility in the interior of the property as often as possible.

Observation #3: Perimeter and Parking Lot Lighting

A lighting survey was conducted as a part of the overall security assessment. Lighting at both the main properties, -------------------- and main campus, was observed to be in need of improvement. One the greatest deterrence to criminal activity around the perimeter and in the parking areas is adequate and bright lighting. Several lights appeared to be out at the main campus in the parking area, around the structure itself, and pedestrian walkways. Even where the lights were fully functional, they appeared to be dim.

Recommendation #3: Improve Lighting

A full scale survey of lighting needs to be performed to identify any lights in need of repair or replacement.* ABC would recommend that the lights that are currently blown be replaced, and future planning include brighter-type lights in the parking area and the perimeter of the building.

*ABC account management is in the process of inventorying all lights and those in need of repair. This will be submitted to -------------------- Hospital upon completion.

Observation #4: Officer Training

Most state relicensing surveys, and hospitals accredited by the Joint Commission on Accreditation of Healthcare Organizations (JCAHO) requires that the security staff must be able to demonstrate a competent workforce that supports the efforts of safety within the environment of care. Hospital security officers, like the clinical staff, must be ready to prove, explain, and demonstrate such competencies.

While we believe that the training program utilized for ABC employees assigned to -------------------- Hospital is currently adequate, we would like to implement even more specialized training in the future. ABC will work toward establishing a more formalized and uniformed process in our ongoing training curriculum to encompass additional areas.

Recommendation #4: Provide Comprehensive Pre-Hire and Ongoing Training, Review/Update Post orders

ABC would recommend that at a minimum all security officers receive a course of prehire and on-going training that encompasses the following.

Observation #5: Hospital Staff Training

It was noted during the assessment tour that additional security awareness training is needed among the hospital staff. -------------------- Hospital has done an excellent job in preparing the staff for many routine situations (fire drills, etc.), but like most organizations, there is a need to expand the awareness levels as it relates to increased workplace security threats.

Recommendation # 5: Increase Staff Security Awareness

Security should be discussed with all hospital staff during the orientation process and other regular training opportunities throughout the year. These topics should include: Active Shooter Response, Workplace Violence Prevention and Response, Employee Theft, and Emergency Response procedures. This training is best conducted by the security staff with coordination among the various hospital departments. ABC is willing to assist with this effort by holding education sessions with employees and/or assisting you in designing an internal education program. (More detail on Active Shooter training is included in this assessment report.)

Observation # 6: Emergency Codes

-------------------- *hospital currently utilizes the following emergency codes:*

Recommendation #6: Provide Increased Training on Codes, and/or Consider the Use of Plain Language Codes Associated with Violence on the Property

While it is to be expected that most employees will not have instant recall of what each code refers to, due to the volume of information (this is addressed by having the codes printed on the badge), the most pressing issue is what response is required, recommended, or preferred when the codes are announced. Of course, some codes are more serious than others. Code silver, for example, may require immediate and deliberate action depending on the situation at hand. Any hesitation could cause the loss of life, or generate chaos among the staff, patients, and visitors.

While some codes do not require a clear and immediate understanding from the general public (such as code orange), others would be relevant to each person on the hospital grounds. ABC would recommend that in conjunction with further active shooter and workplace violence training mentioned elsewhere in this report, -------------------- Hospital consider the use of plain language emergency warnings.

Observation #7: Keypads

Many entrances and sensitive areas are equipped with keypads to allow access to only authorized personnel. While keypads do offer an increased level of protection, they can also present some security issues. It was noted that codes are rarely changed and there is no practical way to prevent unauthorized users. Codes can also be observed from bystanders/visitors. There is also no ability to prevent terminated employees, contractors, or other persons who may have knowledge of the access codes from continuing to access the area after their authorization has ended.

Recommendation # 7: Change Code at Regular Intervals

Access codes should be changed occasionally and after any high-profile terminations. In future planning, it is recommended that more access points and sensitive areas within the hospital be equipped with card access readers. This will give the hospital the ability to strictly control access to areas by "deactivating" access for former employees, and to limit access by time and area for current employees, if needed.

SPECIFIC OBSERVATIONS/RECOMMENDATIONS
Main campus/surrounding properties

The following recommendations are offered to enhance the overall security program:

Observation #1: Patient Watches (Mental Health)

The hospital currently experiences frequent mental health admissions. These patients are under the supervision of the ED security officer, or other security personnel while in other areas of the hospital. Security officers will perform observation on mental health patients when the patient is deemed to be a potential threat, or has exhibited some aggressive behavior. It was noted during the assessment that there is no specified area of the hospital for this purpose. While it is obvious that this is being done out of necessity, and it is not always logistically possible for hospitals to have a floor or area dedicated to mental health treatment, certain precautions should be taken when housing patients under a mental evaluation hold.

One area that was noted during the assessment was the decontamination room. This area has been the site of at least one patient escape. Currently, the exterior of door of this is being secured with a series of ties connected to a garbage can. This was done to "slow down" anyone attempting to escape the decontamination shower.

Recommendation #1: It is recommended that the zip ties attached the garbage can outside of decontamination area be removed and the door secured.

Where possible, make the patient watch rooms more conducive for potentially combative/suicidal patients. Remove anything in the room that can be used as a weapon, harden up the windows, utilize paper sheets, etc. All security officers should also be trained on proper techniques for observing mental health patients.

Observation # 2: Emergency Department

As in any healthcare environment, the -------------------- Hospital Emergency Room presents the greatest risk to staff, patients, and visitors. More than half of the 3465 health workers surveyed by the Emergency Nurses Association reported that they'd been hit, spat on, or physically assaulted while on the job. Nearly a quarter said that they'd experienced 20 or more acts of physical abuse during the previous 3 years. The US Occupational Safety and Health Administration estimates that there are 2600 nonfatal assaults on hospital staff each year. This number is likely higher due to the widespread incidents that are never reported. The overwhelming majority of ER violence is committed by the patient or his/her family members. The American College of Emergency Physicians recently updated their guidelines calling on hospitals to "provide a best-practices security system including adequate security personnel, physical barriers, surveillance equipment, and other security components."

One of the risks posed by the current ED layout is free access to all areas of the hospital from this access point. An internal door has been contructed to prevent this, but it was noted that the public restoroom facilites and vending machines are located beyond this door.

Recommendation #2: Enhanced Emergency Department Procedures

The current -------------------- Hospital security staff has made a concerted effort to improve the presence of security in the ER with a permanent post. This has resulted in fixed post in this area and a directive to spend as much time as possible in and around the emergency department. Whenever possible, this officer should be restricted to the ER entrance and admitting area, unless they are needed to respond to other areas of the department. This officer would also act as a visible access control deterrent to afterhours visitors to the hospital.

ER Visitor Procedures

ABC recommends that -------------------- Hospital establish a formal policy/procedure for visitor and patient access to the ER. This should include an officer greeting the patients/visitors upon entering, and assisting with unloading when necessary. Any visitors wishing to go beyond the waiting area into the Emergency Department treatment area should be given a badge with the name of the patient and the date of arrival. No more than two badges should be issued to visitors per patient. Badges should only be issued after the patient has completed the ER admittance process. Security Officers can be given computer access to a patient roster and print out the visitor's badges using a simple software program, or this can be done by hand after receiving the info from the ER admittance desk. Ideally, the security desk should be placed inside the waiting area, but due to limited space, it is not recommended that the desk be moved from its current location. The following should be posted at or near the entrance to the ER:

- Only Two Visitors Per Patient Inside Treatment Area
- Visitors Passes Issued by Security at This Desk
- No One Under the Age of 12 Admitted Unless They Are a Patient
- No Weapons Allowed in Emergency Room

A Sample Badge containing the required information:

VISITOR

DOE, JOHN

4-1-2015

Visitors should be allowed to alternate the use of the badges and no restrictions should be placed on who the "2" visitors are at a given time – unless they appear to pose a potential threat or disturbance. This will allow the security officer and the ER staff to maintain a sense of control and order by limiting the number of visitors at any given time. The staff should be given discretion to modify this policy if circumstances warrant, but this should be rare and infrequent.

It was also noted during the assessment that the public (ED patients and vistors) will be allowed to use the restrooms located within the ER treating area. While this is not ideal, it is more desirable than allowing free access into the hospital after hours. It is recommended that the vending machines also be moved to within the ER space.

Observation #3: Panic Alarms

Several areas of the hospital are equipped with a panic button (alarm) that can be activated in the event of an emergency. One such area that was observed was in the pharmacy. Employees present in the pharmacy during the assessment seemed to be aware of the presence of the panic button, and also seemed to be uncertain as to the procedures and reaction that would follow in the event that it was pressed. The assessor proposed testing the panic alarm on the day of the assessment, but due to uncertainty as to where the alarm would go and the response that would follow, no testing was performed.

Recommendation # 3: Ensure that all panic alarms are in good condition and operate properly. All employees working in areas that are equipped with panic alarms should be thoroughly trained on how and when to use them and the expected response. Panic alarms should be tested periodically to ensure that they perform when needed.

Observation #4: Unattended Buildings

During the tour of the buildings and departments around the hospital property, the assessment team frequently encountered unattended lobbies and unlocked front doors. In the majority of areas, we were unchallenged and observed what we assume may have been files that contained sensitive medical, confidential, or human resources information. One such example is the physician's surgery center. On the day of the assessment, no one was present on the first floor or the third floor. Only signs directing the visitors and patients where to go. Upon reaching the third floor, it was observed that no one was present and office doors were standing open. Files, documents, and other assorted paperwork were left in plain view and were accessible.

Recommendation #5: When outlying buildings or offices are unattended, some type of access control should be implemented. At minimum, the employees should be trained not to leave their desk or area unattended unless the door is locked or some other means of access control is present. This is especially critical when sensitive or confidential information is present.

Observation #6: Exterior Doors Not Secured/Inoperable

During the assessment, it was noted that several exterior doors at the main campus were being left unlocked and accessible from the outside. When the assessor asked about the procedures for many of the doors, the response was "the door should remain locked at all times." But upon further inspection, many doors were either not locked or were not capable of being locked effectively due to some mechanical defect, in need of repair. The most serious example of this was the hazardous waste storage area adjacent to the loading dock. The door was unlocked and the room was observed to contain hazardous medical waste and other critical materials.

Two other doors were found to be open during the assessment. These were the dock door in the rear of the women's center that contained the nitrous oxide control panel and the door leading into the surgical building/wound care that appeared to be in need of repair to ensure it would close properly (took several attempts to get it to close properly).

Recommendation #6: Repair All Doors That Are Not Operating Properly

ABC would recommend a thorough survey of any and all exterior doors and repairs that are needed. Employees in sensitive areas should be advised to lock the doors when they are not in continuous use.

Assessment location – -------------------- street

The overall presence of security at this location is positive. During the assessment, the security officer was located at the front desk and greeted the team upon arriving. This facility primarily exists as an outpatient/inpatient rehab center and addiction program. A large part of the property is unoccupied. There are two security officers posted around the clock at this location. Their primary duty is to remain at the front desk and make occasional foot patrols around the property. There is no vehicle assigned to security at this location.

Observation #1: Area Needs to be Well Lit

Due to the number of unoccupied dwellings, the criminal potential of the surrounding neighborhood, and the open design of the campus, lighting is a key deterrent at this location. It was observed during the assessment that the area is not well lit in the rear area and the parking areas.

Recommendation #1: Include, in future plans, additional lighting for the perimeter of the building and in parking areas.

Observation #2: Officers Would be More Effective Utilizing a Golf Cart for Patrol

It was noted during the assessment that officers make frequent foot patrols of the entire property. While this is extremely important and serves as a deterrent, a visible golf cart with amber light would be much more effective due to the size of the property and the need for more visibility.

Recommendation #2: Include, in future plans, a golf cart, or a similar type vehicle, at this location.

Active shooter planning and response

No security issue causes as much concern, and security planning challenges, than dealing with the potential of an active shooter on campus. While physical security, officer visibility, and other security procedures are important factors, employee awareness remains the key.

The very nature of healthcare institutions may contribute to violence within the workplace. Many healthcare institutions operate 24 hours a day, 7 days a week; contain a largely female workforce; and maintain reduced staffing levels during the off-hours.

Other environmental contributors include:

■ The prevalence of handguns and other weapons among patients, their families or friends

■ The increasing use of hospitals by police and the criminal justice system for criminal holds and the care of acutely disturbed and violent individuals

■ The increasing number of acute and chronic mentally ill patients being released from hospitals without follow-up care

■ The availability of drugs or money at hospitals, clinics, and pharmacies, making them likely robbery targets

■ Factors such as the unrestricted movement of the public in clinics and hospitals as well as long waits in emergency or clinic areas that lead to client frustration over an inability to obtain needed services promptly

■ Isolated work with clients during times of examinations or treatment

■ Solo work, often in remote locations with no backup or way to get assistance, such as communication devices or alarm systems (this is particularly true in high-crime settings)

■ Stressful work environment

■ Failure to recognize and respond to warning signs such as behavioral changes, mental health issues, personal crises, drug or alcohol use, and disciplinary action or termination, can elevate the risk of a staff member becoming violent toward a patient

■ Failure to report inappropriate, intimidating or bullying behavior that can evolve into threatening or violent incidents

Training is the essential element of any successful workplace violence-reduction program. Many healthcare institutions, however, provide no training or train only limited staff in the art of violence prevention. All staff working within the healthcare field should be required to successfully complete a violence-prevention training program. The training should not be limited to only clinical staff. All administrative and support service staff should be trained as well. The training should be conducted as soon as employment starts, and then made available annually so that the employees can maintain their violence-prevention skills.

ABC recommends that -------------------- Hospital implement a violence prevention/active shooter response plan, and provide comprehensive training to its employees. ABC can assist in this effort by designing a plan and/or providing staff with the appropriate training.

Attached to this report is a sample training program on combatting violence and responding to an active shooter,

GENERAL RECOMMENDATIONS

The following are the general recommendations that we feel may enhance the current overall security program at --------------------:

- Prepare and/or update your emergency procedures dealing with severe weather, crimes in progress, workplace violence, bomb threat response, etc.
- Train all employees (especially supervisory personnel) on fundamental security concepts such as Workplace Violence Prevention, Active Shooter Response, Emergency Response, and Employee Theft.
- Include a section on security in each orientation session for new employees.
- Ensure that all ID badges and parking permits are retrieved from terminated employees prior to them leaving the property.
- Post orders should be reviewed and revised as necessary, at least annually.
- A Security Gap Analysis should be conducted annually and the deficiencies should be corrected.
- Foster relationships with the local law enforcement and encourage a consistent presence (offer free or discounted meals to attract officers on all shifts).

SUMMARY

As noted in the recommendations above, it appears that there are several areas of vulnerability at each facility. One of the keys in improving the overall security plan is improving officer visibility and presence. ABC stands ready to provide you with further information, and to assist in implementing the recommendations contained herein.

If you need further explanation on the recommendations noted, or if you desire a more in-depth assessment, please feel free to contact us.

APPENDIX D

The following is a standard internal litigation hold letter that can be utilized to notify the company employees of the need to secure and preserve evidence in preparation for potential litigation. In addition to internal communications, outside counsel on either side may also send notifications to the company management, warning them not to destroy or lose track of the key documents and information.

Litigation Hold Letter

Dear,

ABC Company has reason to believe that litigation may result from the claim of [name of claimant] that [brief description of potential claim]. Or ABC Company has learned that [name of litigant] has filed a lawsuit for [brief description of claim]. ABC is now under a legal duty to preserve all evidence, whether printed or electronic that might become relevant to this matter. Some of this information may be in your possession or control, and as an ABC employee, you have a legal duty to preserve that information. The purpose of this letter is to explain to you what that obligation means.

You are required to take the following steps immediately to protect and preserve any of that information that is in your possession or under your control, until further notice. Specifically, you will need to do the following immediately:

1. Suspend deletion, overwriting, or any other destruction of electronic information relevant to this dispute that is under your control. This includes electronic information wherever it is stored – on your ABC-owned computer, on a laptop, or at home. It includes all forms of electronic communication, for example, email, word processing, calendars, voice messages, videos, photographs, and information on iPads and smartphones. This electronic information must be preserved so that it can be retrieved at a later time. You can be assured that nothing will be produced for the other side without first being appropriately reviewed and private or privileged information removed. The information must be preserved in its original electronic form, so that all information contained within it, whether visible or not, is also available for inspection, that is, it is not sufficient to make a hard copy of electronic communication. The IT department will attend to the preservation of electronic information on the server and on back-up tapes, if that is called for. Your responsibility is for the information that is under your control.
2. Similarly, preserve any new electronic information that is generated after you receive this letter that is relevant to this dispute.

3. Preserve any hard copy under your control.
4. Immediately notify me if you locate any previously unknown information or documents and forward the same to my attention.

This is an important legal duty and failure to follow these instructions may subject you to discipline, as the failure to preserve this information has very serious consequences for the company.

Please feel free to contact me at any time if you have any questions about this matter or your responsibilities to preserve this vital information.

Thank you for your cooperation.

Sincerely,

Human Resources Manager or Legal Department

APPENDIX E
POSTINCIDENT INVESTIGATIVE CHECKLIST

The following checklist should be utilized to start an investigative file after an incident that could give rise to litigation. In some situations, this list may not be exhaustive as other documents or evidence may need to be gathered or maintained.

POSTINCIDENT INVESTIGATIVE CHECKLIST

Contracts: Secure a copy of the contract in effect at the time of the occurrence. This may be in the form of written agreement signed by both parties, or a purchase order or similar document. If applicable, always check with the local branch office to ensure that you have the most relevant and recent agreement.

Post Orders: Secure a copy of the post orders in effect at the time of the occurrence. This should include any modifications communicated through emails from the customer, memos posted at the worksite, or recorded in pass-down logs.

Daily Activity Reports: Secure copies of all daily activity reports for the location in question, and the date of the occurrence. (It is also a good practice at this point to make sure that the reports prior to and after the occurrence are being maintained as well.)

Incident Reports: Secure copies of all the incident reports. If the officer did not complete an incident report, or the report is not adequate, have those involved make written statements describing their activities prior to, during, and after the occurrence. It is also a good practice to question those who are involved, to elicit information that may not be found within the written reports.

Patrol Recording Data: Inquire about the presence of any tour-recording device that may show where the officer was prior to, during, and after the occurrence.

Witness Statements: Secure witness statements from anyone that may have observed the actual occurrence, or related activities. If the witnesses are employees of your customer, seek permission from the customer representative prior to contacting any witnesses.

Video Footage: Inquire about the presence of video recording in the area of the occurrence or in the surrounding environment. Secure a copy of the recording when possible. Just as with witness statements, in most cases, customer permission will be needed prior to accessing any video storage system.

Payroll Records: Print out or store payroll records showing the times and dates on which officers worked. This should include the date of the occurrence with all shifts (before and after). It is also a good practice to not only print out the prepared schedules, but also secure the actual time records showing who reported for duty.

Media Coverage: If applicable, keep copies of press coverage related to the occurrence. This is also an excellent time to remind all involved of the internal policy on media relations. Remember that any statements made can come back to haunt you later in the process. I have also seen comments made by the customer or other parties to the media that could assist in our defense. Always direct communication to a designated corporate representative with media training. Nothing is worse for public relations, and a potential legal defense, than the picture of an officer running away from TV cameras or making the wrong statement that implies that there is a scandalous secret lurking behind the scenes. It is always tempting to respond to inaccuracies in an effort to repair any damaging information spread by the media, but simple phrases such as "We are currently investigating the incident to determine what occurred and will be taking appropriate steps when the investigation is concluded" or "We are in the process of reviewing the lawsuit and will be responding through the proper legal channels" are advisable in many situations.

Police Reports: Get copies of police reports, if applicable. These reports often contain valuable information that would not otherwise be obtainable through other means. This can include witness information, time of occurrence, who made the initial call to law enforcement, and factors such as interactions with the security officer.

Personnel Files: Secure copies of the personnel files of all officers involved. Also, take this opportunity to self-audit your training programs and hiring process. Regardless of whether or not it appears that the officers were at fault, evaluate compliance with your internal hiring standards to see if all appropriate steps were taken prior to hire and assignment. Check to see if the proper training was conducted during orientation and on-the-job training at the site. Also verify that the officer possessed the correct license and that it is current.

Customer Correspondence: Save all the emails, letters, and other forms of communication between your company and the customer concerning the incident. Make sure that the insurance company remains aware of any request that is made to you from the customer, or the customer's counsel, such as wanting a claim update or seeking a decision on the claim reimbursement. This should include any communication from the customer's insurance company as well.

APPENDIX F

INTRODUCTION TO OUTSIDE COUNSEL

The following is an initial checklist to use when preparing for your initial meeting with an outside counsel who has been retained to represent the security company. Other information may need to be shared, but this is offered as a baseline for what details should be communicated to set the tone for the on-going relationship.

- Brief History of Your Company: Include ownership, number of employees, office and service area locations, and customer base served.
- Brief description of security officer industry in general.
- State and/or local licensing regulations regarding the security officers. Also provide information concerning the required training and background checks that all officers must go through.
- Internal company policies on hiring and on-going training.

APPENDIX G
INITIAL DOCUMENT LIST FOR ATTORNEY REPRESENTING THE SECURITY COMPANY

The following is the list of the documents and information that should be presented to the attorney who has been retained to represent the security company.

- Brief history of the contractual relationship between the security company and the customer. This should include any and all security assessments or recommendations that may have been provided by the security company over the life of the contract.
- Information concerning any similar prior incidents at the location in question.
- Personnel files of the officers involved, highlighting any prior disciplinary or background issues.
- A description of the training provided to the officers involved, as well as documented training records.
- Written post instructions for the location in question, or if unavailable, a description of what duties were expected to be performed.
- All current contractual agreements between the customer and the security company.
- Any and all other documents relevant to the action such as daily activity reports, incident reports, statements, and witness information.

APPENDIX H
DEPOSITION TIPS AND TECHNIQUES

I have been given several practical tips on surviving depositions that are universal and effective. While every session is unique, following these proven steps can assist greatly in improving your deposition performance.

Always tell the truth – this may seem obvious, and you may find it insulting for someone to suggest that you would do otherwise. However, this advice is not offered to anyone who is contemplating being dishonest. Let's face it, if they're willing to think about lying, someone telling them not to, is not going to do much to sway them. This is for those individuals who may consciously, or subconsciously, add or remove facts because they feel the actual answer is not appropriate or comprehensive enough. I've seen this quite often when witnesses are asked about specific dates. I'm always amazed when witnesses quote exact dates and times when asked during depositions. Sometimes, I will find out later that they were merely agreeing with the attorney for fear of looking foolish for not knowing, are turning an estimation into a purported fact rather than simply admitting they did not know.

Listen to the question – most witnesses are filled with anxiety and nerves. And because they have often been over prepared with aggressive techniques, the witnesses are almost preprogrammed to expect certain questions. This can result in the witness actually answering the question before it is even asked. During my preparation of witnesses I often tell them that I can reasonably anticipate some of the questions are going to be asked, but there are a multitude of others that I may not know are coming. One of the best pieces of advice I was given for my deposition was to keep your mouth shut until the attorney finishes with the question and make sure that you understand it before you start your answer. There have been many times that I was certain that I would be asked a series of questions that never came up. I am sometimes strangely disappointed that I will not get to use the information I have prepared, but I have learned that if they don't ask, I don't answer.

Make certain that you understand the question being asked – there is a natural tendency for witness to want to avoid looking as if they are unqualified to be there. This can result in a witness attempting to answering questions they think they were asked as opposed to the ones that are actually being presented. I must confess that in my younger days, I would give plaintiff attorneys fits by pouncing on any perceived flaws in their wording or improper phrasing used by a plaintiff's attorney. I considered it my chief goal to make the other side ask me the right question before I would grace them with my answer. But my attempts to be evasive aside, there are often times when there are genuine misunderstandings about the questions that are asked. Witnesses should never be intimidated to the point where they feel they cannot ask for a question to be clarified before answering. Most plaintiff attorneys will even be appreciative that you are taking the time to point out that there may be some confusion about what's being asked.

Answer only the question you are asked – there's probably nothing that the plaintiff's attorney likes more than a witness who gives long and detailed answers in depositions. In my estimation, there are two extremes of witnesses: (1) those who give almost exclusively "yes" and "no" answers and refuse to expound on any particular topic and (2) those who give 20-min speeches regardless of how simple the inquiry is. I was preparing a security officer for a deposition related to a crime that had occurred at a customer facility. I had told the officer that at some point he should be prepared to explain his many years of experience in the security industry and the numerous training classes he had attended during his career. When the time for his deposition arrived he was ready to perform. He was asked to state his name and his response not only included that information but also a 5-min recitation of his security officer experience and training classes that he had attended. The plaintiff's attorney had to ask him to stop talking so that he could ask the second question – which was "what is your current address?"

Use plain, simple language – this may come as a revelation, but most attorneys taking your deposition, and certainly others that may hear or read it later, are not well-versed in all matters relating to private security. Ignorance of this fact can cause the witness to inadvertently speak in industry lingo and use words and phrases that are difficult to understand. I have been stopped many times and asked to explain what I meant by certain phrases or words because I was the only person in the room who knew what "I" was talking about. Security professionals and witnesses in general can also fall into the trap of thinking that the more elevated the language, the more effective the testimony will be; this is rarely true. Remember, even though depositions are not routinely seen by juries or judges, they can be. Assume that your audience knows nothing about your industry and your experiences. Instead of saying that you recommended the "additional deployment of a nonlethal uniformed security countermeasure," it will make the day much shorter to simply explain that you proposed to the customer that another unarmed security officer be placed on the property.

Take your time – in depositions, and even more so at trial, a minute can feel like an eternity. Witnesses can be made to feel that the answers should be given immediately without any delay. Add the ominous presence of a video camera a few feet from your face, and this can cause the average person to feel that they must spit out a quick answer in order to appear responsive. But there is nothing wrong with taking a couple of moments to consider an answer that may not be subject to immediate recall. When dealing with documents, don't hesitate to ask to take another look, or to be given a minute to read.

Do not take guesses – witnesses in depositions can sometimes feel as if they are required to be preprogrammed robots who must have a succinct answer for every question posed. Otherwise, why are they there? It is actually okay not to remember something, or not to recall minute details about a very specific date, time, or even an event. Now I am not talking about the stereotypical image of the shadowy political figure who is hauled before a congressional committee and answers 90% of the Senator's questions with "I don't recall," but rather those times in depositions where you're being pressed for a specific answer and you frankly don't have one. There's a very real tendency to create what you think the answer may be and then offer it as your best guess, disguised as a "fact'" If you want to qualify an answer with uncertainty, do so. "I cannot recall the exact date of the meeting, but I believe it was sometime in early 2014" is a much better answer than "yes, you're right the meeting did take place on January 5th."

Don't allow yourself to get boxed in – boxing in involves asking a question in such a way that it will be difficult for the witness to testify differently later in the deposition, or at trial. I have been boxed in numerous times before, and it can happen very easily if the witness is not on guard against this tactic. One clear signal is questions that begin with the phrase, "would you agree that …"followed by an alleged statement of facts concerning a key element in the case. I am asked routinely in security litigation cases to agree with the statement that "when performed competently and professionally security officer services will deter and prevent criminal activity." Sounds harmless enough, but a quick and reassuring "oh yes of course" response from the witness can lead into several damning follow-up questions. My somewhat standard response to that garden-variety question is typically "security officer services are designed to deter certain activity, but prevention is something that is extremely difficult to quantify, and the presence of a security officer, or even a law enforcement officer for that matter, would not be seen by any reasonable person as an absolute guarantee that no criminal activity will occur."

Don't argue – I must admit this is the one that I personally struggle with when giving depositions. What makes this particularly difficult to overcome, is the fact that occasionally you are dealing with someone who prefers to conduct depositions in an argumentative manner. I am not the one who likes to paint with a broad brush when it comes to attorneys, and I have been fortunate to be deposed by some of the most respectful and courteous professionals in the legal world, but I certainly have had my experience with what I refer to as "blowhards." These attorneys feel that intimidation is the most-effective tactic when questioning a witness. When giving depositions, I have been accused of withholding evidence, making false statements under oath, and been subjected to the implication that I had no sympathy for the victim. Remain confident, purposeful, and calm and you will be much more effective.

APPENDIX I
TRIAL TESTIMONY TIPS AND TECHNIQUES

The following are general tips and techniques for being an effective witness at an actual trial:

Always tell the truth – At trial, as in all other matters, honesty is the best policy. If you tell the truth and tell it accurately, nobody can cross you up. Do not guess or make up an answer. If you do not know the answer, it is best to say, "I don't know." If you are asked about details that you do not remember, it is best to say, "I don't remember."

Be attentive. – You should remain alert at all times so that you can hear, understand, and give a proper response to each question. If the judge or jury get the impression that you are bored or indifferent, they may tend to disregard your testimony.

Take your time and speak clearly and loudly. – Give the question such thought as it requires to understand it. The juror farthest from you should be able to hear distinctly what you have to say. Since all testimony is recorded, do not nod your head "yes" or "no."

Answer all questions directly. – Answer only the questions asked, then stop. Avoid "volunteering" information. If you do not understand a question, ask that it should be explained. Do not look at the lawyer for help while you are testifying and never ask the Judge if you have to answer. You are on your own. This will give the jury the impression that you are holding something back.

Be serious in the courtroom. – Avoid joking and wisecracks in the jury's presence. This includes hallway actions and conversations.

Do not lose your temper. – Remember that some attorneys may attempt to wear you down so that you will lose your temper and say things that are not correct. Hold your temper and your testimony will be much more valuable. Do not fence or argue with the attorneys. They have a right to question you, and many are expert in this craft.

Stay Away from Traps. – If you make an estimate, make sure that everyone understands that you are estimating. Be cautious of the questions asking if you are willing to swear to your version of the events. You were "sworn" to tell the truth when you took the stand, do not be afraid of saying so. Beware of questions asking you if another witness was telling the truth or lying. You can only tell the truth based upon your observations. You have no way of knowing what another person observed, especially when you did not hear that person testify.

Give positive, definite answers when at all possible. – Avoid saying, "I think, I believe, In my opinion." A witness testifies to facts, not beliefs, or opinions. Do not say, "That's all that happened." Cover yourself, and say, "That's all I recall." Later in your testimony, you may remember more details.

Be yourself – Do not use *"legalese"* or security *"lingo"* just for the sake of impressing the jury. It will have the opposite effect.

The most effective witness is the one who can tell their story comfortably. Just tell the truth and be yourself. Everything else will take care of itself.

APPENDIX J

The following sample discovery documents are taken from actual cases involving security companies in the area of negligent security. It follows upon the fictional case of Litigation Lane Apartments and ABC Security. They are offered as a representation of what you may be faced with in the area of discovery during a related case.

Sample interrogatories

1. Please identify yourself by stating your full name, present address, date and place of birth, Social Security number, and the name of your spouse.
2. Please state the name and address of any potential party to this lawsuit, not already named as a party hereto.
3. Please state how your business relationship with Litigation Lane Apartments began and on what date. If there is a contract, or any other document memorializing this relationship, please provide a copy.
4. Please state whether or not you are aware of the policy against allowing any nonresidents to gain access to Litigation Lane Apartments property. If your answer is in the affirmative, please state fully what this policy was.
5. Please describe in detail what services you provide as it pertains to crime prevention services as advertised on your website. Please also list dates, times, and attendance rosters for any crime prevention classes you held during the time you were providing services to Litigation Lane Apartments.
6. Please describe in detail any security evaluations, risk assessments, crime analysis, or any other study you undertook before or during the time you provided security services to Litigation Lane Apartments. Please include any recommended security measures that were provided to Litigation Lane Apartments prior to you commencing security services.
7. Please list all of the professional organizations ABC Security Company holds membership in. Please also list any certifications or other professional designations.
8. Please provide a copy of all marketing material, standard proposals, or other advertising related to your crime prevention services.
9. Please provide a list of all customers over the 5 years immediately preceding the vicious attack on the plaintiff that occurred on January 1, 2015, whereby any type of workplace violence or violent criminal activity occurred. Please include in your response the name of the

customer, address, type of criminal or violent incident, and the date of such incident.

10. Please state whether or not there was any video surveillance at the south end of Litigation Lane Apartments on January 1, 2015. If so, please state whether or not you are in custody and control of said video, or if you have knowledge of who would be in custody and control of said video.

11. Please state the name, position, and current employment status of each and every person employed by ABC Security who was working at Litigation Lane Apartments for the 6-month period immediately preceding the vicious attack on the plaintiff that occurred on January 1, 2015.

12. Please describe in detail your internal hiring process including recruitment, screening, and training.

13. Please describe in detail how ABC Security Company was first notified of the vicious attack suffered by the plaintiff on January 1, 2015.

14. Please provide a detailed listing of any and all criminal activity observed and/or reported by the employees of ABC Security Company that occurred on or around the property known as Litigation Lane Apartments for the 6-month period immediately preceding the vicious attack on the plaintiff that occurred on January 1, 2015.

15. Please state the name of each and every insurance company that may be liable to satisfy, indemnify, or reimburse all or part of the judgment that may ultimately be entered in this action. Please state the dollar amount of any and all liability insurance coverage available in this action.

APPENDIX K
Sample request for documents

1. Please identify yourself by stating your full name, present address, date and place of birth, Social Security number, and the name of your spouse.
2. Please state the name and address of any potential party to this lawsuit, not already named as a party hereto.
3. Please state how your business relationship with Litigation Lane Apartments began and on what date. If there is a contract, or any other document memorializing this relationship, please provide a copy.
4. Please state whether or not you are aware of the policy against allowing any nonresidents to gain access to Litigation Lane Apartments property. If your answer is in the affirmative, please state fully what this policy was.
5. Please describe in detail what services you provide as it pertains to crime prevention services as advertised on your website. Please also list dates, times, and attendance rosters for any crime prevention classes you held during the time you were providing services to Litigation Lane Apartments.
6. Please describe in detail any security evaluations, risk assessments, crime analysis, or any other study you undertook before or during the time you provided security services to Litigation Lane Apartments. Please include any recommended security measures that were provided to Litigation Lane Apartments prior to you commencing security services.
7. Please list all of the professional organizations ABC Security Company holds membership in. Please also list any certifications or other professional designations.
8. Please provide a copy of all marketing material, standard proposals, or other advertising related to your crime prevention services.
9. Please provide a list of all customers over the 5 years immediately preceding the vicious attack on the plaintiff that occurred on January 1, 2015, whereby any type of workplace violence or violent criminal activity occurred. Please include in your response the name of the customer, address, type of criminal or violent incident, and the date of such incident.
10. Please state whether or not there was any video surveillance at the south end of Litigation Lane Apartments on January 1, 2015. If so, please state whether or not you are in custody and control of said video, or if you have knowledge of who would be in custody and control of said video.

11. Please state the name, position, and current employment status of each and every person employed by ABC security who was working at Litigation Lane Apartments for the 6-month period immediately preceding the vicious attack on the plaintiff that occurred on January 1, 2015.

12. Please describe in detail your internal hiring process including recruitment, screening, and training.

13. Please describe in detail how ABC Security Company was first notified of the vicious attack suffered by the plaintiff on January 1, 2015.

14. Please provide a detailed listing of any and all criminal activity observed and/or reported by the employees of ABC Security Company that occurred on or around the property known as Litigation Lane Apartments for the 6-month period immediately preceding the vicious attack on the plaintiff that occurred on January 1, 2015.

15. Please state the name of each and every insurance company that may be liable to satisfy, indemnify, or reimburse all or part of the judgment that may ultimately be entered in this action. Please state the dollar amount of any and all liability insurance coverage available in this action.

Subject Index

Printed in the United States
By Bookmasters